THE COCAINE OF FINANCE
Why Crypto Harms Society, Corrupts Power, and Endangers Ordinary People

ButterflyMan

For permission requests, contact:

ButterflyMan Publishing LLC

Email: contact@butterflyman.com

Website: www.butterflyman.com

This book is a work of nonfiction.

All analysis, interpretations, and opinions expressed herein are those of the author and do not constitute financial, legal, or investment advice.

First Edition — 2025

Printed in the United States of America

ISBN: 979-8-90217-017-4

Book Design: ButterflyMan Publishing LLC

INTRODUCTION

Money That Feels Good, Then Kills Quietly

There is a moment in every social crisis when the language used to describe it becomes more dangerous than the phenomenon itself.

In the case of crypto currency—especially cryptocurrency—that moment has already passed.

For more than a decade, the public has been told a story. A story about innovation. About freedom. About decentralization. About a new kind of money that would liberate ordinary people from banks, governments, and elites. The language has been intoxicating: *trustless*, *permissionless*, *borderless*, *inevitable*. To question it is often framed as ignorance, fear, or hostility to progress itself.

And yet, beneath this language, a very different reality has taken shape.

Ordinary people are losing their life savings through scams they cannot understand and losses they cannot reverse. Elderly citizens—who have done nothing more than trust a familiar voice or a friendly face—are being systematically targeted and financially destroyed. Criminal networks have discovered the most efficient transfer rail in history. Corruption has found a new hiding place. And democratic legal systems, built on traceability and accountability, are struggling to respond to a system designed to avoid both.

This book begins from a simple, uncomfortable premise:

> **Crypto currency is not merely a risky investment. It is a socially corrosive financial product whose harms now outweigh any plausible benefit to ordinary people.**

To say this clearly, without euphemism or ideology, is the purpose of this book.

Why This Is Not an Anti-Technology Book

It is important to say at the outset what this book is *not*.

This is not an argument against technology.
It is not an argument against the internet, encryption, software, or innovation.
It is not a defense of inefficient banks or corrupt institutions.

On the contrary, many of the technologies that underlie modern digital life—real-time payments, secure databases, cryptographic verification, distributed computing—are not only useful but necessary for a functioning modern society.

The problem is not digital technology.

The problem is **what happens when a speculative, irreversible, and unprotected financial system is marketed to the public as money**.

Innovation is not defined by novelty.
It is defined by **whether it makes life safer, more predictable, and more humane for the majority of people who must live with it**.

By that standard, crypto currency—particularly cryptocurrency as it exists today—has failed.

Why Ordinary People Are Always the Victims

One of the most persistent myths surrounding crypto currency is that those who lose money are simply careless, greedy, or irresponsible. This belief is comforting to those who profit from the system, because it shifts blame away from design and onto victims.

This book rejects that framing entirely.

Modern societies do not function by requiring every citizen to become a technical expert. We do not ask people to audit electrical grids before turning on a light. We do not require them to understand pharmaceutical chemistry before taking prescribed medicine. We do not expect them to reverse-engineer banking infrastructure before depositing a paycheck.

We build systems **precisely so ordinary people can use them safely without specialized knowledge**.

Crypto currency breaks this social contract.

To participate safely, users are expected to understand:

- irreversible transactions,
- private key custody,
- phishing attacks and impersonation,
- fake exchanges and fake wallets,
- smart-contract exploits,
- cross-chain laundering mechanisms.

Failure at any step can result in **total, permanent loss**, with no institution capable of intervention.

This is not empowerment.
It is abandonment.

And it is why the victims of crypto currency are not primarily sophisticated traders or engineers, but **ordinary people whose trust is weaponized against them**.

The Pattern We Refuse to See

Across countries, cultures, and political systems, the same pattern repeats:

1. Crypto currency is introduced as innovation.
2. Early adopters and insiders profit disproportionately.
3. Complexity increases faster than understanding.
4. Scams proliferate where reversibility does not exist.
5. Criminal actors adapt faster than regulators.
6. Ordinary people absorb losses.
7. Public trust erodes.
8. Institutions respond after the damage is done.

At no point does this pattern depend on individual morality. It is structural.

If this pattern described a pharmaceutical drug, it would be withdrawn from the market.
If it described a consumer product, it would be banned.
If it described a food additive, it would be regulated as toxic.

But because it is framed as "finance" and "technology," the harm is tolerated.

That tolerance is the true scandal.

The Metaphor of Financial Cocaine

This book uses a metaphor that may feel uncomfortable, but is analytically precise:

Crypto currency functions in society the way cocaine functions in the body.

Cocaine is not dangerous because it is immediately unpleasant. It is dangerous because:

- it feels empowering at first,
- it creates the illusion of control,
- it bypasses natural regulatory systems,
- it produces dependency,
- it externalizes harm,
- and it leaves long-term damage that far exceeds the short-term pleasure.

Similarly, crypto currency:

- feels like freedom,
- promises autonomy,
- bypasses institutional safeguards,
- concentrates gains early,
- spreads harm widely,
- and leaves devastation that cannot be reversed.

No serious society treats cocaine as a matter of "personal responsibility" alone. We recognize that some products are **too harmful to be normalized**, regardless of individual choice.

The central argument of this book is that **crypto currency has crossed that threshold**.

Why This Crisis Is Getting Worse, Not Better

Some readers may believe that crypto currency's problems are transitional—that better regulation, better education, or better technology will solve them.

This book argues the opposite.

The more crypto currency is normalized:

- the larger the victim pool becomes,
- the more effective scams become,
- the more entrenched criminal usage becomes,
- the harder legal enforcement becomes,
- and the more corrosive the long-term effects on governance and trust.

What began as a fringe experiment has now reached:
- national politics,
- institutional finance,
- public pensions,
- elder communities,
- and international crime networks.

At this scale, **design flaws become societal hazards**.

Power, Politics, and the Collapse of Warning Systems

One of the most dangerous accelerants of harm is political legitimization.

When leaders signal that crypto currency is acceptable, innovative, or strategically important—without simultaneously building consumer protection—the public interprets that signal as safety approval.

Warnings from law enforcement lose credibility. Skepticism collapses. Scammers gain a powerful narrative: *If the system were dangerous, surely it would not be endorsed.*

This book examines how political power, when combined with an already dangerous financial system, can transform private risk into **public catastrophe.**

What This Book Will Do

This book does not ask readers to take a leap of faith. It does not rely on ideology, conspiracy, or fear-mongering.

Instead, it will:

- Explain **what money is**, and why crypto currency fails that definition.
- Show **how Ponzi-like dynamics emerge without a single promoter**.
- Document **how ordinary people are systematically harmed**.
- Analyze **crime, corruption, and geopolitical misuse**.
- Examine **political legitimization and its consequences**.
- Present **data-driven comparisons before and after normalization**.
- Argue for **a public-health approach, including prohibition**.
- Offer **a vision of a safe digital future without crypto**.

This is not a call for nostalgia.
It is a call for **responsibility**.

The Choice in Front of Us

Every generation inherits technologies it did not invent and must decide whether to normalize, regulate, or reject them.

The question this book poses is simple but profound:

Do we want a financial system that feels empowering to a few, or one that is safe for the many?

If we choose the former, the damage will continue quietly, relentlessly, and unevenly—until trust itself becomes collateral.

If we choose the latter, we must be willing to say what few are willing to say:

Some products are too harmful to belong in public life.

Crypto currency is one of them.

TABLE OF CONTENTS

FULL BOOK STRUCTURE

INTRODUCTION

Money That Feels Good, Then Kills Quietly
- Why "innovation" language hides harm
- Why ordinary people are the victims
- Why this is not anti-technology but **pro-society**
- The "financial cocaine" metaphor explained

PART I — WHAT CRYPTO CURRENCY REALLY IS

Chapter 1 — Crypto Currency Is Not Money
- No unit of account
- No stability
- No consumer protection
- Speculation masquerading as currency

Chapter 2 — Ponzi Dynamics Without a Promoter
- Early adopters
- Exit liquidity
- Narrative economics
- Why "belief" replaces value

Chapter 3 — Complexity as Predation
- Why normal people cannot understand crypto
- Why this is not their fault
- Information asymmetry as extraction

PART II — HOW ORDINARY PEOPLE ARE HARMED

Chapter 4 — Dating Scams, Investment Traps, and Irreversible Loss
- Pig-butchering schemes
- Fake platforms
- Psychological manipulation

PART IV — POWER, POLITICS, AND LEGITIMIZATION

Chapter 10 — When Presidents Legitimize Dangerous Money
- Executive signaling
- Mixed messages
- Collapse of public warning systems

Chapter 11 — Trump, Crypto, and the Risk of Political Normalization
- Family involvement as legitimacy signal
- Pardons and moral hazard
- Congress and regulatory weakening
- Why supporters are most at risk

Chapter 12 — When Dark Finance Merges with State Power
- Scenario analysis
- Public safety collapse
- Corruption normalization
- Shadow governance

PART V — DATA, FUTURES, AND SYSTEMIC RISK

Chapter 13 — Before and After: What the Data Shows
- Market volatility
- Scam loss baselines
- Enforcement lag
- Exposure expansion

Chapter 14 — Futures We Should Fear
- Mainstream without safety
- Politicized volatility
- Shadow finance integration

PART VI — WHAT MUST BE DONE

Chapter 15 — Banning Crypto as a Public Health Measure
- "Financial cocaine" framework
- Why partial regulation fails

Chapter 16 — The Right Path to a Ban
- Retail prohibition
- On-ramp shutdown
- Liability
- Reversibility

Chapter 17 — A Safe Digital Future Without Crypto
- Digital payments ≠ crypto
- Banking modernization
- Real innovation

CONCLUSION

Choosing Protection Over Addiction
- What kind of society we want
- Why freedom requires guardrails
- Why some products must be banned

APPENDIX 01
Presidential Crypto Signaling and Public Safety

How Political Legitimization Can Amplify Crypto Scams, Weaken Consumer Warning Systems, and Increase Governance Risk

APPENDIX 02
A Legal–Institutional Analysis of Crypto Legitimation in Democratic Systems

Presidential Signaling, Crypto Currency, and Public Safety Risk

APPENDIX 03
SCENARIO PLANNING MEMO (FOR POLICYMAKERS)

Public Safety Risks at the Intersection of Crypto Currency and Executive Power

APPENDIX 04
A Data-driven risk memo that compares "before vs after presidential involvement"

APPENDIX 05
Policy Path to Ban Crypto Currency for Public Safety Treating Retail Crypto Like a High-Harm Product

PART I — WHAT CRYPTO CURRENCY REALLY IS

Chapter 1 — Crypto Currency Is Not Money

Section 1 — What Money Is (and Why This Definition Matters)

Before judging whether crypto currency is good or bad, innovative or dangerous, one question must be answered clearly and without ideology:

What is money?

Money is not whatever people speculate on.
It is not whatever technology makes transferable.
And it is not whatever price happens to go up.

Money is a **social institution**, not a commodity.

Across history and across cultures, functioning monetary systems—regardless of political ideology—share four non-negotiable functions:

> 1. **Unit of account** – a stable measure of value
> 2. **Medium of exchange** – widely accepted for everyday transactions
> 3. **Store of value** – preserves purchasing power reasonably over time
> 4. **Institutional protection** – backed by dispute resolution, reversibility, and legal accountability

These are not academic preferences.
They are **survival requirements for complex societies**.

When any one of these functions collapses, the damage is not theoretical. It appears as:

- mispricing,

- fraud,
- inequality,
- social distrust,
- and eventually political instability.

This is why no serious society allows "experimental money" to circulate freely among the public without strict safeguards.

Digital currency fails this test—not marginally, but fundamentally.

Section 2 — Crypto Currency Fails as a Unit of Account

A unit of account is the quiet backbone of everyday life.

It allows people to answer basic questions:

- How much does this cost?
- Is it affordable?
- Is it fair?
- Is it profitable?

For a unit of account to function, **relative stability is essential**.

Cryptocurrency has none.

Bitcoin, Ethereum, and most tokens exhibit volatility that routinely exceeds:

- 10% in a single day,
- 30–50% in weeks,
- 70–90% across cycles.

This volatility is not a temporary "adoption phase."
It is structural.

Prices are driven by:

- speculative flows,
- leverage,
- narratives,
- political signaling,
- influencer amplification.

They are not driven by:

- productivity,
- wages,
- consumption,
- real output.

No household can plan.
No business can price.
No contract can be trusted.

A system that cannot measure reality **cannot organize society**.

Section 3 — Medium of Exchange: Where the Myth Collapses

Crypto advocates often claim crypto currency is a superior medium of exchange: fast, global, frictionless.

This argument collapses the moment it meets reality.

In real economies:

- wages are paid in national currency,
- taxes are collected in national currency,
- rent, utilities, healthcare, and food are priced in national currency.

Cryptocurrency is not widely accepted because:

- merchants cannot absorb volatility,
- accounting is complex and risky,
- chargebacks do not exist,
- fraud exposure is extreme.

Where crypto *is* widely used as a medium of exchange, it is disproportionately associated with:
- illegal markets,
- ransomware payments,
- scam settlement rails.

A medium of exchange that ordinary people cannot use safely is not innovation.
It is **exclusion**.

Section 4 — The Missing Function: Protection, Reversibility, and Trust

If crypto currency failed merely because it was volatile or speculative, it might still be repairable. Financial history contains many examples of unstable assets that were eventually stabilized through regulation, institutional backing, and social learning.

What makes crypto currency fundamentally unfit as money is something far more severe:

the deliberate removal of protection and reversibility.

Modern financial systems are not built on the assumption that people are perfectly rational or technically competent. They are built on the opposite assumption: **humans make mistakes**.

That is why banks can reverse fraudulent transfers.
That is why credit card networks allow chargebacks.
That is why courts can freeze assets.
That is why deposits are insured.

22

These mechanisms do not exist to encourage irresponsibility. They exist because **without error correction, mass participation becomes dangerous**.

Cryptocurrency systems reject this logic entirely.

In most crypto systems:

- transactions are irreversible by design,
- mistakes are permanent,
- fraud is final,
- theft is functionally indistinguishable from user error.

Advocates describe this as "freedom" and "personal responsibility."
In institutional terms, it is the **removal of money's immune system**.

A monetary system without reversibility does not produce trust.
It produces fear, silence, and concealment.

Section 5 — Why Irreversibility Is Not a Feature but a Catastrophe

Irreversibility is often marketed as a virtue. Users are told that once transactions cannot be undone, money becomes "pure," "final," and "sovereign."

This framing is profoundly misleading.

Irreversibility is only beneficial in environments where:

- all participants are highly trained,
- identities are stable and verifiable,
- fraud rates are low,
- dispute resolution exists elsewhere.

Retail finance satisfies none of these conditions.

For ordinary people, irreversibility means:

- a single phishing message can destroy a lifetime of savings,
  - one wrong click ends all legal remedies,
  - embarrassment prevents reporting,
  - and recovery is impossible.

In traditional finance, fraud is treated as a **system failure**. In crypto, fraud is reframed as a **personal moral failure**.

This shift is not accidental. It externalizes cost away from system designers and onto victims.

A financial system that treats irreversible loss as a pedagogical tool is not educational.
It is predatory.

Section 6 — Trust Is Not Removed; It Is Shifted and Weaponized

Crypto advocates often claim that cryptocurrency "removes trust."

This is false.

Trust is not eliminated; it is merely **relocated**.

Instead of trusting:

- regulated institutions,
  - legal systems,
  - dispute mechanisms,

users must trust:

- wallet software,
- anonymous developers,
- opaque codebases,
- online communities,
- unverifiable platforms.

This is not trust minimization.
It is **trust displacement**—from accountable institutions to unaccountable actors.

The result is not decentralization.
It is **diffuse irresponsibility**.

When something goes wrong, there is no counterparty, no authority, and no remedy. Responsibility evaporates precisely when it is needed most.

Section 7 — Complexity as a Structural Advantage for Insiders

Crypto currency systems are often defended as "open" because the code is public. This confuses theoretical accessibility with practical accessibility.

In reality, effective participation requires:

- deep technical literacy,
- constant vigilance,
- and exposure to rapidly evolving attack vectors.

This creates a permanent information asymmetry.

Those who design and promote the system:

- understand its fragility,
- know where risks concentrate,

- and exit before collapse.

Late entrants do not lack intelligence.
They lack **inside position**.

This is why losses are socially concentrated downward
while gains concentrate upward.

Complexity is not neutral here.
It functions as an extraction mechanism.

Section 8 — Why Crypto Currency Was Never Built for Ordinary Life

No mass social movement demanded:

- irreversible money,
- anonymous finance,
- extreme volatility,
- zero consumer protection.

Crypto currency did not emerge to solve:

- healthcare affordability,
- housing insecurity,
- wage stagnation,
- education access.

It emerged to solve a different problem:

how to move value without accountability.

That problem is highly relevant to:

- criminals,
- speculators,
- sanction evaders,
- and political actors seeking opacity.

26

It is not relevant to ordinary households.

This mismatch explains why criminal adoption preceded mainstream adoption—and why it remains structurally dominant.

Section 9 — Money Without an Immune System

Healthy financial systems behave like living organisms. They detect anomalies, respond to threats, and repair damage.

Cryptocurrency systems do not.

They lack:

- fraud antibodies,
- corrective reflexes,
- and institutional memory.

They reward speed over caution and finality over fairness.

This is why crypto currency behaves less like money and more like a **financial narcotic**:

- providing short-term euphoria,
- suppressing risk perception,
- and producing long-term systemic damage.

Section 10 — Conclusion: If It Is Not Money, What Is It?

Crypto currency is not money in any functional, social, or institutional sense.

It does not:

- measure value reliably,
- facilitate everyday exchange safely,

- preserve purchasing power,
- or protect participants from predictable harm.

What it does is enable:

- speculation,
- opacity,
- extraction,
- and irreversible loss.

Calling it "money" is not innovation.
It is mislabeling with consequences.

And when a society mislabels a high-risk speculative system as money, the damage does not remain financial. It becomes social, legal, and political.

That is why this book begins here.

Chapter 2 — Ponzi Dynamics Without a Promoter

When Belief Replaces Value

1. Why Crypto Does Not Look Like a Ponzi — and Why That Makes It More Dangerous

When people hear the term *Ponzi scheme*, they usually imagine a familiar figure: a central operator who promises steady returns, pays early participants with money from later ones, and eventually collapses when inflows dry up.

Cryptocurrency advocates rely heavily on this mental image when dismissing criticism. They say, correctly in a narrow sense:

> "Crypto cannot be a Ponzi, because there is no central promoter."

> Formally, this statement is true.
> Substantively, it is irrelevant.

> The most dangerous financial structures in history have not always been driven by a single fraudster. They have often emerged from **self-reinforcing incentive systems**—markets where no one needs to lie explicitly, because the structure itself produces extraction.

> Cryptocurrency belongs to this category.

> It does not require a promoter, because **the system performs the role of the promoter**.

2. The Core Question: Where Do Returns Come From?

All investment systems can be reduced to one foundational question:

What is the source of returns?

In productive economic systems, returns come from:

- increased productivity,
- profits generated by firms,
- services rendered,
- interest derived from real economic activity.

Cryptocurrencies, as a class, generate **no intrinsic cash flow**.
They do not represent claims on earnings.
They do not entitle holders to dividends.
They do not correspond to productive output.

The overwhelming majority of crypto "returns" come from one source only:

Someone else buying the same asset later, at a higher price.

This is not a moral judgment. It is a mechanical description.

That mechanism is indistinguishable from the core logic of a Ponzi structure:
value flows **from later entrants to earlier ones**, rather than from production to investors.

3. Early Entrants and the Architecture of Advantage

Time is not neutral in crypto markets.
It is a form of power.

Early entrants benefit from three structural advantages:

Cost Asymmetry

Early participants acquire tokens at negligible cost relative to later prices. Even dramatic crashes often leave them profitable.

Information Asymmetry

They are closer to developers, insiders, narrative creators, and liquidity providers. They understand risks earlier—and exit earlier.

Liquidity Asymmetry

They can sell into hype-driven markets, while later entrants must absorb volatility and illiquidity.

Late entrants are not less intelligent.
They are simply **structurally disadvantaged**.

This asymmetry is not incidental—it is essential to the system's functioning.

4. Exit Liquidity: The Term That Explains Everything

Within crypto markets, there is a term that is rarely explained to the public but universally understood by insiders:

Exit liquidity.

Exit liquidity means this:

> *Your ability to profit depends on someone else being willing to buy when you sell.*

That buyer is almost always:

- newer,
- less informed,
- more emotionally driven,
- more exposed to loss.

Crypto markets do not create value.
They **reassign loss over time**.

Every realized gain requires an unrealized loss elsewhere.

5. Narrative Economics: When Stories Replace Fundamentals

In traditional finance, narratives supplement fundamentals.
In crypto, narratives **replace** them.

Price movements are justified not by earnings or productivity,
but by slogans:

- "This is the future."
- "Institutions are coming."
- "Adoption is inevitable."
- "You don't understand it yet."
- "This time is different."

These narratives share three traits:

- they are not falsifiable,
- they are not measurable,
- they carry no accountability.

When prices rise, the story is validated retroactively.
When prices fall, the story mutates.

Narrative elasticity substitutes for economic substance.

6. The Moralization of Holding and the Stigmatization of Exit

Because the system depends on continued belief, behavior must be shaped culturally.

As a result:

- holding becomes a moral virtue,
- selling becomes betrayal,
- skepticism becomes ignorance,
- losses become "lessons."

This is not investment culture.
It is belief enforcement.

Rational risk management is reframed as weakness, while loyalty to the asset is framed as character.

This dynamic mirrors religious and cult-like structures more than financial markets.

7. Why This Is Not Free Market Choice

A free market requires:

- informed participants,
- comprehensible risks,
- reversible errors,
- survivable failure.

Crypto markets offer none of these conditions to ordinary participants.

Instead, they operate under:

- radical information asymmetry,
- extreme technical opacity,

- irreversible loss,
- and social pressure to participate.

Participation under these conditions is not free choice.
It is **structural inducement**.

8. Scaling the Structure: From Individual Loss to Social Harm

At small scale, Ponzi-like dynamics destroy individuals.
At large scale, they destroy **trust**.

As crypto expands:

- scam ecosystems professionalize,
- influencers monetize belief,
- political actors legitimize exposure,
- risk warnings are drowned out.

When collapse occurs:

- no central actor is accountable,
- no restitution is possible,
- losses are socialized downward.

This is the hallmark of systemic extraction.

9. Why the Absence of a Promoter Is the Greatest Risk

Traditional Ponzi schemes eventually end because someone can be prosecuted.

Crypto has no such pressure valve.

There is no operator to arrest.
No fund to unwind.
No balance sheet to distribute.

Responsibility dissolves into protocol, community, and ideology.

A system without a responsible party is not decentralized safety. It is **distributed irresponsibility**.

10. Conclusion: A Self-Expanding Ponzi Structure

Cryptocurrency does not require deception to function as a Ponzi-like system. Its incentive architecture performs the work automatically.

It rewards:
- early entry,
- loud promotion,
- narrative amplification.

It penalizes:
- caution,
- delay,
- skepticism.

When belief replaces value, when narratives replace cash flow, and when later entrants become the source of earlier gains, the underlying structure becomes clear—regardless of how modern the technology appears.

That clarity is essential, because without it, the harm will continue to scale invisibly.

Chapter 3 — Complexity as Predation

Why Ordinary People Can Never "Learn" Crypto

1. The False Promise of Education

When confronted with the scale of harm caused by cryptocurrency—scams, irreversible losses, and widespread confusion—defenders almost always reach for the same explanation:

> "People just need better education."
>
> This response is comforting. It implies that the system itself is sound, and that harm results only from ignorance. If people would simply read more, learn more, and become more careful, the damage would disappear.
>
> This belief is wrong.
>
> Cryptocurrency does not fail because people are insufficiently educated.
> It fails because it **requires a level of technical vigilance that no mass society can sustain**.
>
> The problem is not a lack of learning.
> The problem is **structural complexity**.

2. Complexity Is Not Neutral

In theory, complexity is often framed as a challenge that can be overcome with effort. In practice, complexity functions as a **sorting mechanism**.

In systems with low complexity:

- mistakes are correctable,
- risks are visible,
- participation is broad.

In systems with high complexity:

- errors compound,
- risks are opaque,
- insiders dominate outcomes.

Cryptocurrency belongs decisively to the second category.

Complexity here is not accidental.
It is **the operating condition of the system**.

3. What "Learning Crypto" Actually Requires

To participate safely in cryptocurrency, an ordinary user must understand and continuously monitor:

- private key custody and backup protocols,
- wallet software security and update risks,
- phishing attacks and social engineering tactics,
- fake exchanges and cloned interfaces,
- smart contract vulnerabilities,
- bridge exploits and cross-chain risks,
- tokenomics, liquidity pools, and slippage,
- regulatory uncertainty across jurisdictions.

Failure at any single point can result in **total and permanent loss**.

This is not a learning curve.
It is a **continuous exposure surface**.

No other consumer financial product imposes this burden.

4. The Myth of the Competent Retail User

Crypto discourse is filled with an idealized figure: the competent, disciplined, technically fluent retail user who manages private keys flawlessly and avoids all traps.

This figure does not exist at scale.

Modern societies are built precisely on the recognition that:

- people are busy,
- attention is limited,
- trust is necessary,
- mistakes are inevitable.

Financial systems exist to absorb these realities, not punish them.

A system that works only for the hyper-vigilant minority is not inclusive innovation.
It is **designed exclusion**.

5. Asymmetry by Design

Complex systems always advantage those who design, maintain, and monitor them.

In crypto:

- developers understand attack surfaces,
- insiders know when risks escalate,
- exchanges control information flow,
- early adopters exit before collapse.

Late entrants face a system that is already hostile to them.

This is not a coincidence.

It is the predictable result of **information asymmetry embedded in technical design**.

When complexity and irreversibility coexist, losses will always concentrate downward.

6. Education Cannot Solve Adversarial Environments

Crypto markets are not neutral learning environments.
They are **actively adversarial**.

Scammers do not wait for users to learn.
They adapt faster than any public education effort.

For every safety guide published, there are:

- new phishing formats,
- AI-generated impersonations,
- cloned wallets and exchanges,
- social engineering scripts refined by criminal networks.

Education assumes a stable environment.
Crypto operates in a **permanently hostile one**.

Teaching people to survive in such an environment is not empowerment.
It is exposure.

7. The Burden Shift: From System Responsibility to Individual Blame

One of the most damaging consequences of complexity is moral reframing.

When people lose money in traditional finance, investigators ask:

- Where did the system fail?
- What safeguards were missing?
- How can recurrence be prevented?

In crypto, the dominant question becomes:
- Why wasn't the user careful enough?

This shift absolves designers, platforms, and promoters of responsibility, while placing impossible expectations on individuals.

A system that blames victims for predictable failure is not innovative.
It is **ethically inverted**.

8. Why This Is Predation, Not Participation

Predation does not require malicious intent at every level.
It requires a structure where harm is foreseeable, recurring, and profitable.

Crypto satisfies all three conditions.
- Harm is foreseeable because complexity and irreversibility guarantee failure at scale.
- Harm is recurring because new users continually enter.
- Harm is profitable because losses become someone else's gains.

Calling this "participation" obscures the reality.

This is **extraction through complexity**.

9. Why Ordinary People Can Never Catch Up

The final illusion is that ordinary users will eventually "catch up" as technology matures.

But crypto complexity does not decline over time—it increases.

- New layers are added.
- New tokens proliferate.
- New chains fragment liquidity.
- New attack vectors emerge.

There is no end state where the system becomes simple, stable, and safe for mass use—because **simplicity would eliminate its speculative edge.**

A system that depends on complexity to function cannot be simplified without collapsing its incentives.

10. Conclusion: Complexity as a Gate, Not a Bridge

Cryptocurrency does not democratize finance.
It **re-stratifies it**.

Those with time, expertise, and inside access survive.
Those without them are exposed to irreversible loss.

Complexity here is not a bridge to inclusion.
It is a **gate that closes behind early entrants**.

When a financial system requires ordinary people to become full-time risk managers just to avoid ruin, it has already failed its social purpose.

That failure is not educational.
It is structural.

PART II — HOW ORDINARY PEOPLE ARE HARMED

Chapter 4 — Dating Scams, Investment Traps, and Irreversible Loss

How Crypto Turns Human Trust into a Weapon

1. Crypto Did Not Invent Fraud — It Industrialized It

Fraud is not new. Societies have always had scammers, con artists, and confidence games. What is new is the **infrastructure** that cryptocurrency provides.

Traditional financial systems impose four natural constraints on fraud:

1. **Traceability** — money leaves records.
2. **Reversibility** — transactions can be halted or undone.
3. **Intermediary liability** — banks and platforms have legal duties.
4. **Jurisdictional reach** — courts can freeze assets.

Cryptocurrency systems invert all four:
- anonymity or pseudo-anonymity,
- irreversibility by design,
- removal of accountable intermediaries,
- and frictionless cross-border movement.

This is not technology being "misused."
It is technology **optimized** for fraud.

2. Pig-Butchering Is Not an Accident — It Is the Optimal Scam

Among crypto frauds, so-called *pig-butchering* schemes are not peripheral. They are **structurally optimal**.

The logic is simple:

- crypto transactions are irreversible,
- technical complexity prevents verification,
- investment and speculation blur together,
- social platforms provide low-cost access to targets.

The scam evolves accordingly:

1. **Trust formation** (romance, friendship, shared values),
2. **Gradual financial introduction** ("I just want to help you"),
3. **Manufactured expertise** (screenshots, fake dashboards),
4. **One large irreversible transfer**,
5. **Simultaneous disappearance of money and relationship**.

Crypto is not merely a tool in this sequence. It is the **decisive enabling condition**.

3. Why Intelligent, Disciplined People Fall Victim

The most cruel and persistent myth surrounding fraud victims is this:

"They were foolish."

Large-scale fraud does not rely on stupidity.

It relies on **normal human psychology**:

- trust,
- hope,
- shame,
- emotional attachment.

Crypto scams are effective because they:

- combine emotional manipulation with technical opacity,
- isolate victims from verification,
- and ensure that once loss occurs, it is final.

Ironically, people who are rational, patient, and emotionally invested over time can be **more vulnerable**, not less.

4. Fake Platforms and the Power of Visible Illusion

Most crypto investment scams do not ask victims to send money directly to a scammer. Instead, victims are guided to **professional-looking platforms**:

- realistic trading interfaces,
- live-updating prices,
- account balances that appear accessible,
- initial small withdrawals to establish credibility.

This stage is psychological, not technical.

The goal is to make victims **see** their money growing.

Once belief is anchored, rationalization takes over:

- "I verified it myself."
- "I saw the profits."
- "This isn't blind trust."

The final large transfer then becomes inevitable.

5. Irreversibility Turns Loss into Long-Term Trauma

In traditional fraud cases, victims retain at least some hope:

- asset freezes,
- chargebacks,
- court action.

In crypto fraud, hope is removed **at the protocol level**.

Once a transaction occurs:

- funds are rapidly fragmented,
- routed through mixers and bridges,
- and moved beyond practical legal reach within minutes.

What remains is not just financial loss, but **psychological injury**:

- shame,
- self-blame,
- distrust of others,
- withdrawal from institutions.

Many victims remain silent, masking the true scale of harm.

6. Law Enforcement Is Not Failing — It Is Being Bypassed

A common defense is that fraud persists due to weak enforcement.

This misreads the reality.

In crypto scams, law enforcement is often excluded **by design**:

- jurisdictional fragmentation,
- anonymous infrastructure,
- absence of accountable intermediaries,
- irreversible execution.

This is not enforcement failure.
It is **legal evasion as architecture**.

7. When Fraud Scales, Social Trust Collapses

When scams become industrialized, consequences extend beyond individual victims.

Over time:

- strangers become threats,
- intimacy becomes monetized,
- elderly and immigrant populations are systematically targeted,
- families fracture under shame and secrecy.

Crypto fraud does not merely redistribute money.
It **erodes the social fabric**.

8. Why "Be More Careful" Is Not a Solution

Public advisories often end with calls for vigilance.

This is inadequate and irresponsible.

No functioning society expects ordinary citizens to:

- operate with counter-intelligence-level suspicion,
- master complex financial technology,
- distrust intimate relationships as default.

47

A system that requires permanent hyper-vigilance to avoid ruin is not viable.

9. Who Pays for the Damage

The costs of crypto fraud are not borne by:

- platforms,
- promoters,
- system designers.

They fall on:
- families,
- elderly savers,
- migrants,
- socially isolated individuals.

These losses convert into:

- public assistance burdens,
- healthcare and mental-health costs,
- declining trust in institutions.

Markets do not absorb these losses.
Societies do.

10. Conclusion: When Finance Treats Humanity as a Vulnerability

Crypto-enabled fraud succeeds not because people are weak, but because the system **treats humanity as an exploitable surface**.

When a financial architecture:

- relies on trust without protection,
- encourages participation without responsibility,
- rewards extraction while blaming victims,

it crosses from innovation into **systemic harm**.

At that point, the question is no longer whether the technology is impressive, but whether society should tolerate it at all.

Chapter 5 — The Elderly as the Primary Target

Trust, Technical Gaps, and the Silence That Follows

1. Targeting Is Not Random — It Is Strategic

The overrepresentation of older adults among cryptocurrency fraud victims is not accidental. It reflects **rational targeting by criminals operating within a permissive system**.

Elderly individuals tend to possess:

- accumulated lifetime savings,
- predictable income streams,
- a higher propensity to trust authority and relationships,
- lower familiarity with rapidly evolving digital systems.

Crypto-enabled fraud does not seek ignorance; it seeks **asymmetry**. Age amplifies that asymmetry.

2. Trust as a Social Asset — and a Point of Exploitation

Trust is not a weakness. In functioning societies, it is a social asset cultivated over decades. Older adults grew up in financial environments where:

- banks were stable institutions,
- fraud was exceptional rather than systemic,
- disputes could be resolved,
- and transactions could be corrected.

Cryptocurrency collapses these assumptions without replacing them with equivalent safeguards.

What was once prudent trust becomes, in this new context, a liability.

3. The Technical Gap Is Not a Knowledge Gap

The common explanation for elderly vulnerability focuses on "digital literacy." This framing is misleading.

The issue is not that older adults fail to understand technology. It is that **the technology demands unrealistic levels of continuous competence**.

Crypto systems require users to:

- secure private keys perfectly,
- identify subtle interface manipulations,
- distinguish authentic platforms from replicas,
- react quickly under pressure,
- and recover from zero mistakes.

This is not a reasonable expectation for any demographic—let alone those whose cognitive load increases with age.

4. Authority Mimicry and Manufactured Legitimacy

Scams targeting older adults often rely on **authority simulation**:

- impersonation of financial advisors,
- references to government approval,
- fabricated regulatory language,
- claims of institutional endorsement.

Cryptocurrency's ambiguous legal status enables this tactic. When boundaries are unclear, imitation flourishes.

Victims are not defying warnings. They are responding rationally to signals that appear legitimate within a deliberately confusing environment.

5. Shame as a Secondary Weapon

Loss is only the first injury.

The second is shame.

Older victims frequently experience:

- fear of appearing incompetent,
- guilt over "wasting" family resources,
- reluctance to disclose losses,
- withdrawal from financial decision-making.

This silence benefits criminals and obscures the true scale of harm.

When victims disappear quietly, systems face no pressure to change.

6. Family-Level Consequences

Crypto fraud rarely ends with the victim.

Consequences cascade:

- adult children absorb financial burdens,
- family trust erodes,
- caregiving resources are diverted,
- intergenerational conflict intensifies.

These are not market externalities.
They are **social costs imposed without consent**.

7. Why Warnings Fail Older Populations

Public warnings often rely on:

- technical explanations,
- rapid-response advisories,
- abstract risk framing.

These approaches fail older adults because they assume:

- constant media monitoring,
- familiarity with digital threat models,
- willingness to distrust all outreach.

Effective protection would require **structural prevention**, not individual vigilance.

8. The Moral Failure of "Personal Responsibility" Narratives

Blaming elderly victims for "falling behind" technologically is ethically indefensible.

Modern finance has always adapted to human limitations. That adaptation is a mark of progress, not weakness.

A system that demands perfection from its most vulnerable participants is not empowering.
It is **predatory**.

9. Demographic Risk Concentration and Public Cost

As populations age, the risk profile worsens:

- more assets concentrate among older cohorts,
- more fraud targets become available,
- more losses shift to public assistance systems.

Crypto does not merely exploit existing vulnerability.
It **scales it**.

10. Conclusion: When a System Feeds on Trust

The defining characteristic of crypto-enabled elder fraud is not deception alone—it is **betrayal of social expectations**.

When a financial system:

- leverages trust without honoring it,
- exposes those least able to recover,
- and then disappears behind technical finality,

it ceases to be a neutral market phenomenon.

It becomes a **systemic transfer from dignity to damage**.

Chapter 6 — Why "Personal Responsibility" Is a Lie

How Crypto Abandons the Social Contract

1. "Personal Responsibility" Is Not a Neutral Moral Principle

In debates about cryptocurrency, "personal responsibility" is repeatedly invoked as a moral shield.

When someone loses life savings to a scam, the response is:

> "They should have been more careful."

> When a user makes a single mistake and loses everything, the response is:

> "That's the price of decentralization."

> When systemic risk is raised, the response is:

> "Freedom means accepting consequences."

> These statements appear mature and principled.
> In reality, they function as **a rhetorical weapon**.

> In the crypto context, "personal responsibility" is not used to assign accountability—it is used to **erase institutional responsibility**.

2. The Core Achievement of Modern Finance Was Protection, Not Permission

To understand why this narrative is dishonest, we must recall why modern financial systems exist.

Banks, payment rails, consumer protections, insurance mechanisms, and regulators were not created to:

- coddle the public,
- eliminate risk,
- or reward irrational behavior.

They were created around a hard-earned insight:

Large-scale societies cannot function on the assumption of perfect human behavior.

Modern finance treats:
- error as inevitable,
- fraud as systemic risk,
- and protection as a prerequisite for participation.

This is not a rejection of responsibility.
It is the **institutionalization of responsibility**.

3. Crypto's Responsibility Model: Infinite Liability, Zero Protection

Cryptocurrency inverts this logic completely.

It imposes:

- **unlimited individual liability**
- alongside **near-total absence of institutional protection**.

In crypto systems:
- one mistake can mean permanent ruin,
- one deception ends all recourse,
- one error nullifies decades of savings.

At the same time:
- designers face no duty of care,

- platforms disclaim liability,
- promoters evade accountability,
- and losses are non-recoverable by design.

This is not responsibility.
It is **responsibility displacement**.

4. When Risk Is Individualized, Extraction Becomes Legitimate

Redefining systemic risk as personal failure has a clear consequence:

Extraction becomes morally defensible.

If losses are framed as "your choice," then:

- platforms have no obligation to improve safety,
- promoters face no consequence for misinformation,
- policymakers face no urgency to intervene.

The system's incentives remain intact—and expand.

This is not a free market.
It is **institutionalized negligence**.

5. Why This Logic Is Rejected Everywhere Else

Consider how this argument would sound in other domains:
- A drug released without trials, justified as "consumer choice."
- An aircraft built without redundancy, justified as "passenger responsibility."
- Food sold without regulation, justified as "buyer beware."

These positions are absurd in any mature society.

Finance is no different.
Because financial failure:
- propagates beyond individuals,
- amplifies inequality,
- and produces public cost.

Crypto is treated as an exception not because it is safer—
but because it is framed as ideology.

6. Responsibility Does Not Mean Punishing the Vulnerable

True responsibility does not mean transferring all risk to those
least able to bear it.

Responsibility means:

- designers answer for foreseeable harm,
- platforms protect users by default,
- promoters bear consequences for deception,
- states intervene when risk becomes systemic.

A system that punishes victims while insulating risk
creators is not empowering.
It is **predatory**.

7. "Voluntary Participation" Does Not Eliminate Duty of Care

Crypto advocates often argue that participation is voluntary.

This ignores reality.

Participation occurs in environments defined by:

- extreme information asymmetry,

- systematic risk minimization,
- relentless social pressure,
- and constant authority signaling.

Consent obtained under manipulation does not eliminate responsibility.

Clicking "I agree" does not dissolve the social contract.

8. The Collapse of the Modern Financial Contract

The implicit contract of modern finance is simple:

**Individuals bear limited risk;
institutions bear systemic risk.**

Cryptocurrency shreds this contract.

It demands total exposure from individuals while rejecting collective obligation.

This is not progress.
It is **regression to pre-modern finance**, where ruin was personal and irreparable.

9. The Political Function of Responsibility Rhetoric

The persistence of the "personal responsibility" narrative is not accidental.

It serves a political function:

- justifying regulatory inaction,
- normalizing public harm,
- insulating power from scrutiny.

When failure is individualized, systems escape accountability.

10. Conclusion: When Responsibility Is Used to Deny Responsibility

In the crypto ecosystem, "personal responsibility" has been inverted.

It no longer restrains power.
It protects power.

When a financial system:

- disguises systemic risk as personal choice,
- reframes protection as weakness,
- and humiliates victims as cautionary tales,

it has abandoned the ethical foundations of modern society.

That abandonment is not incidental.
It is the precondition for the corruption, crime, and political capture that follow.

PART III — CRIME, CORRUPTION, AND DARK FINANCE

Chapter 7 — Crypto as the Perfect Crime Rail

Drugs, Ransomware, Organized Crime, and Terror Financing

1. Crime Does Not "Adopt" Neutral Tools — It Selects Optimal Ones

Criminal enterprises are pragmatic. They do not adopt technologies because they are fashionable or innovative. They adopt them because those technologies **minimize risk, maximize speed, and evade accountability**.

From this perspective, the embrace of cryptocurrency by criminal networks was not incidental or opportunistic. It was **structurally inevitable**.

A financial rail that is:

- borderless,
- pseudonymous or anonymous,
- irreversible,
- and lightly regulated,

is not merely compatible with crime.
It is **purpose-built for it**.

2. Why Cash Was a Constraint — and Crypto Removed It

For decades, physical cash imposed real limitations on crime:

- bulk was difficult to move,
- storage was risky,
- cross-border transport attracted scrutiny,
- and laundering required exposure to intermediaries.

Cryptocurrency eliminates nearly all of these constraints.

Value can be:

- transmitted instantly across borders,
- split and recombined algorithmically,
- layered through obfuscation tools,
- and stored without physical presence.

What once required complex laundering networks can now be accomplished **by code**.

3. Ransomware: The Clearest Proof of Concept

No criminal use case demonstrates crypto's enabling role more clearly than ransomware.

Before cryptocurrency, ransomware was limited. Attackers had no reliable, scalable way to receive payment without identification.

Crypto changed that.

Ransomware now relies on:

- crypto wallets as payment endpoints,
- automated payment verification,
- instant fund movement,
- and rapid obfuscation post-payment.

This is not incidental usage.
Ransomware is **financially impossible at scale without cryptocurrency**.

The explosive growth of ransomware correlates directly with the availability and normalization of crypto payment rails.

4. Drug Markets and the Industrialization of Illicit Trade

Illicit drug markets did not simply "move online." They were **re-engineered** around crypto.

Cryptocurrency enables:

- escrow systems without accountability,
- cross-border wholesale transactions,
- rapid supplier switching,
- and global retail distribution.

The result is not decentralization—it is **industrialization**.

Markets become:

- more resilient,
- harder to dismantle,
- and faster to regenerate after enforcement action.

Crypto does not just facilitate drug trade.
It **optimizes** it.

5. Organized Crime and the End of Traceability

For organized crime groups, cryptocurrency offers a structural advantage beyond speed: **plausible deniability**.

Funds can be:

- routed through mixers,
- bridged across chains,
- converted into privacy coins,
- and exited through informal or lightly regulated on-ramps.

Even when transactions are technically "on-chain," attribution becomes prohibitively difficult once funds fragment.

This does not eliminate law enforcement—it **overwhelms it**.

6. Terror Financing and Sanction Evasion

Groups under international sanctions face severe restrictions in traditional finance. Crypto offers a partial—but meaningful—workaround.

Cryptocurrency allows:

- small-donor aggregation without banking oversight,
- rapid cross-border transfers,
- reduced dependence on formal institutions,
- and symbolic signaling to supporters.

While crypto does not replace all terror financing channels, it **lowers the barrier to entry** and complicates interdiction.

Similarly, sanctioned states and proxies can use crypto to:

- bypass payment restrictions,
- experiment with alternative settlement,
- and test regulatory limits.

Opacity becomes a strategic asset.

7. Why "Blockchain Transparency" Is a Misleading Defense

A common defense is that blockchains are transparent, and therefore hostile to crime.
This argument collapses under scrutiny.

Transparency without identity is not accountability.

Criminal use exploits:

- pseudonymous addresses,
- layered transactions,
- time delays,
- and jurisdictional gaps.

Public ledgers may record movement, but they do not reliably establish **who controls what**.

In practice, transparency shifts the burden to investigators while criminals adapt faster than attribution methods improve.

8. Enforcement Is Reactive; Crypto Is Adaptive

Law enforcement operates under constraints:

- due process,
- jurisdiction,
- evidentiary standards,
- and finite resources.

Criminal networks do not.

They:

- update tactics rapidly,
- exploit regulatory arbitrage,
- migrate across platforms,
- and test enforcement thresholds continuously.

Crypto accelerates this imbalance.

By the time one method is identified, another has already replaced it.

9. The False Comfort of "Small Percentages"

Crypto defenders often minimize criminal use by citing percentages of total transaction volume.

This framing is deceptive.

Even a small percentage of a large, fast-moving system can represent:

- billions in illicit value,
- continuous criminal revenue,
- and high-impact social harm.

Financial systems are judged not by average use, but by **worst-case amplification**.

Crypto performs poorly under that test.

10. Conclusion: When the Rail Shapes the Crime

Cryptocurrency does not merely support criminal activity.
It **reshapes it**.

It lowers barriers, accelerates scale, and weakens enforcement asymmetrically.

When a financial infrastructure systematically advantages criminals over institutions, the issue is no longer misuse—it is **design**.

A society that tolerates such a rail must confront a difficult truth:

It is not just enabling crime.
It is **restructuring crime in its own image**.

Chapter 8 — Crypto Currency as a Corruption Infrastructure

Public Bribery Without Envelopes, Private Kickbacks Without Invoices

1. Corruption Did Not Disappear — It Was Reengineered

Corruption is not a cultural flaw unique to certain societies. It is a **structural outcome of incentives**. When power is concentrated, oversight is weak, and rewards are large, corruption emerges.

Crypto currency did not invent corruption.
It did something far more dangerous:

> **It transformed corruption from a high-risk, traceable act into a low-risk, scalable technical process.**
>
> When value transfers become anonymous, irreversible, cross-border, and intermediary-free, corruption no longer requires elaborate concealment. It becomes **embedded in ordinary financial flows**.

2. From Envelopes to Addresses: A Structural Shift in Bribery

Traditional bribery carried inherent risks:
- physical exchange,
- identifiable intermediaries,
- observable transactions,
- evidentiary trails.

Crypto currency eliminates these constraints.

A bribe can now take the form of:
- a "private investment opportunity,"

- a preferential token allocation,
- an airdrop,
- or the quiet sharing of a wallet address.

No envelope changes hands.
No meeting occurs.
Yet value is transferred.

The corruption has not vanished—it has **changed form**.

3. The Public Sector: When Power Meets Untraceable Payment

In public governance, crypto currency introduces three decisive advantages for corruption:

Invisibility

Payments appear as market activity rather than illicit transfers.

Temporal Separation

Rewards can be delivered long after decisions are made, evading correlation analysis.

Jurisdictional Escape

Funds can exit national legal reach within minutes.

As a result:
- regulatory leniency,
- selective enforcement,
- policy favoritism,

can be quietly purchased without traditional red flags.

4. The Private Sector: Kickbacks Without Accounting

Corporate corruption historically required:

- false invoices,
- shell contracts,
- accounting manipulation,
- and significant exposure.

Crypto currency replaces this with:

- token-based "consulting fees,"
- pre-allocations labeled as partnerships,
- blockchain transfers disguised as innovation.

There is no invoice.
No audit trail.
No reconciliation point.

Kickbacks no longer look illegal—they look **technical**.

5. Shadow Wealth and Hidden Incentives

When corrupt transfers fragment and digitalize, they create a new phenomenon:

shadow wealth.

This wealth:

- does not appear in bank accounts,
- escapes asset disclosure,
- avoids taxation,
- yet powerfully shapes incentives.

Officials, regulators, executives, and intermediaries may appear compliant while holding **off-ledger financial interests**.

This is not merely individual misconduct.
It is **systemic incentive distortion**.

6. Why Democratic Systems Are Especially Vulnerable

Democratic legal systems rely on:

- transparency,
- traceability,
- evidentiary standards.

Crypto currency erodes all three.

Even when suspicion exists:

- attribution is difficult,
- evidence is fragmented,
- legal thresholds cannot be met.

The result is not the absence of corruption—but the **absence of proof**.

Cases collapse not because misconduct did not occur, but because it cannot be demonstrated within the rule of law.

7. "Innovation" as Ideological Cover

The most effective shield for digital-currency-enabled corruption is not technical—it is rhetorical.

Terms such as:
- "innovation,"
- "financial future,"
- "technology neutrality,"

reframe scrutiny as ignorance and oversight as repression.

Under this framing:
- regulation is depicted as backward,
- investigation as political persecution,
- accountability as hostility to progress.

Corruption gains **ideological camouflage**.

8. From Isolated Acts to Institutional Capture

When such mechanisms scale, corruption ceases to be episodic.

It becomes structural:

- policy aligns with speculative finance,
- public resources are privatized,
- regulations favor narrow interests,
- losses are socialized.

Digital currency shifts from tool to **core infrastructure of incentive alignment**.

9. Why Regulation Alone Often Fails

Some argue that smarter regulation can solve these problems.

This underestimates the design reality.

A system engineered to evade oversight cannot be regulated into transparency.

As long as:
- irreversibility remains,
- anonymity persists,
- cross-border opacity is preserved,

corruption will migrate, mutate, and reconstitute itself.

10. Conclusion: When Corruption Becomes Infrastructure

The gravest danger of digital currency is not volatility.
It is **the silent normalization of unaccountable power-money fusion**.

When bribery no longer needs envelopes,
when kickbacks no longer need invoices,
when incentives leave no trace,

corruption evolves from crime into **systemic risk**.

Any society that tolerates such infrastructure must confront a fundamental question:

Can public trust and rule of law survive when corruption becomes invisible by design?

Chapter 9 — Country and Regional Case Studies

How Crypto Currency Interacts with Power, Crime, and Governance Across Different Political Systems

I. Why National Context Matters

Crypto currency does not operate in a vacuum.
Its real-world impact depends on the **institutional environment** in which it is embedded.

The same technical features—**anonymity, irreversibility, and cross-border mobility**—interact with very different incentive structures across political systems, including:

- authoritarian regimes,
- hybrid political systems,
- mature democracies,
- and developing economies.

This chapter does not rank countries morally.
Instead, it examines a more fundamental question:

> **In which institutional environments does digital currency operate "smoothly,"
> and in which does it amplify pre-existing risks?**

II. North Korea: Cryptocurrency as a Sanctions Survival Tool

North Korea represents the clearest case of **strategic, state-level use of cryptocurrency**.

Facing near-total exclusion from the international financial system, the regime has systematically used digital currency to:

- steal foreign exchange through cyberattacks,
- launder funds across borders,
- finance weapons and missile programs,
- and bypass sanctions enforcement mechanisms.

Multiple public investigations show that state-linked hacking groups have stolen **billions of dollars in crypto assets** through:

- exchange breaches,
- DeFi vulnerabilities,
- and social engineering operations.

For North Korea, cryptocurrency is not a speculative asset. It is a **survival-oriented financial instrument**.

It allows a sanctioned state to participate in global value transfer **without diplomatic recognition, correspondent banking, or transparency**.

This is not a loophole.
It is **institutional bypass**.

III. Russia: Oligarchy, Gray Zones, and Geopolitical Flexibility

In Russia, cryptocurrency has neither been fully embraced nor completely banned.
Instead, it exists in a **deliberately maintained gray zone**.

Its primary functions include:

- providing capital mobility buffers for elites,
- partial sanctions circumvention,
- tolerance or neglect of ransomware ecosystems,
- and informal overlap between criminal networks and state interests.

Although authorities periodically signal regulation or crackdowns, enforcement remains highly selective.

This ambiguity is itself strategic.

Cryptocurrency provides Russia with:

- plausible deniability,
- financial experimentation outside Western systems,
- asymmetric tools in cyber and economic conflict.

The result is a space where **crime, geopolitics, and finance intersect**.

IV. China: Domestic Suppression, External Utilization

China's stance on cryptocurrency is often mischaracterized as total opposition.

In reality, China follows a **dual-track strategy**:

- harsh suppression of domestic retail trading and speculation,
- strict limits on capital flight via crypto channels.

At the same time, certain China-linked actors—whether state-connected or tacitly tolerated—have:
- engaged extensively in early-stage mining,
- participated in global crypto infrastructure,
- used crypto-based laundering and settlement channels abroad.

This approach reflects institutional logic:
- maintaining financial and social control domestically,
- exploiting opacity externally.

China does not treat cryptocurrency as monetary innovation,
but as a **sovereignty risk**—unless it can be controlled or externalized.

V. United States: Normalization, Lobbying, and Retail Exposure

The United States represents a fundamentally different model.

In the U.S., cryptocurrency has been:

- highly financialized,
- aggressively marketed to retail investors,
- politically legitimized through lobbying,
- and partially "normalized" amid regulatory ambiguity.

Key features include:

- large-scale retail losses,
- industrialized scam ecosystems,
- fragmented regulation,
- political signaling that weakens public risk perception.

Unlike authoritarian systems, the U.S. does not adopt crypto for state survival or control,
but for **market expansion and financial gain**.

This creates a paradox:

- high legal standards,
- weak preventive protection,
- widespread social harm,
- unclear accountability.

VI. European Union: Cautious Regulation and Structural Limits

The EU has generally taken a more cautious approach, emphasizing:

- consumer protection,
- licensing regimes,
- and harmonized regulatory frameworks.

However, structural challenges remain:
- uneven enforcement capacity among member states,
- complex cross-border supervision,
- illicit flows migrating toward weaker jurisdictions.

Regulation can mitigate risk,
but it cannot eliminate core features such as:

- irreversibility,
- anonymity,
- rapid cross-border movement.

The EU experience illustrates the **upper limit of regulation**:
risk reduction without full resolution.

VII. Developing Economies: High Exposure, Low Resilience

In developing economies, cryptocurrency is often framed as:

- financial inclusion,
- an inflation hedge,
- a leapfrogging development path.

The reality is different:

- weak consumer protection,
- limited enforcement capacity,
- concentrated scam activity,
- rapid capital outflows.

Crypto does not build local credit systems or productive capacity.
It **accelerates extraction of already scarce resources**.

Losses are ultimately borne by families, communities, and informal safety nets.

VIII. Comparative Findings: A Consistent Structural Pattern

Across systems, a clear pattern emerges:

- **Authoritarian regimes** use crypto as a strategic constraint-evasion tool.
- **Hybrid systems** exploit ambiguity and selective enforcement.
- **Democracies** expose the public through normalization.
- **Developing economies** suffer disproportionate social harm.

The common factor is not ideology,
but **incentive alignment**.

IX. "Global Adoption" as a Misleading Metric

Advocates often cite adoption rates as evidence of success.

This confuses **spread** with **welfare**.

Viruses also spread efficiently.

The relevant questions are not "how many use it," but:

- who benefits,
- who absorbs losses,
- and who can exit safely.

Across these dimensions, outcomes are highly asymmetric.

X. Conclusion: Crypto Currency as a Governance Stress Test

Crypto currency functions as a **governance stress test**.

It amplifies existing weaknesses:

- corruption where oversight is weak,
- crime where enforcement is strained,
- speculation where protection is absent.

It does not reform governance.
It **exposes institutional fault lines**.

Any serious assessment of digital currency must therefore begin with **institutional reality**, not technological fantasy.

PART IV — POWER, POLITICS, AND LEGITIMIZATION

Chapter 10 — When Presidents Legitimize Dangerous Money

Executive Signaling, Mixed Messages, and the Collapse of Public Warning Systems

1. Why Presidential Signals Matter More Than Policy Text

In modern societies, the actions and words of presidents and heads of government do not merely reflect policy—they **shape perceived legitimacy**.

For most citizens:

- regulatory language is abstract,
- technical warnings are distant,
- financial risk is difficult to assess.

But presidential behavior is **interpreted intuitively**.

When a president publicly endorses, tolerates, or associates with a financial instrument, the public does not read footnotes or caveats. They read one message:

"This must be safe enough."

This is not irrational.
It is how authority functions in mass societies.

2. Legitimization Without Safeguards

Danger does not arise only when governments formally legalize risky systems. It often arises earlier—through **legitimization without protection**.

This occurs when:

- political leaders praise innovation without addressing harm,
- executive agencies issue mixed or conflicting signals,
- enforcement is delayed while promotion accelerates.

The result is a regulatory vacuum filled not by caution, but by marketing.

In this environment, risk warnings lose salience, while exposure expands rapidly.

3. Mixed Messages and the Erosion of Public Risk Perception

Public warning systems depend on clarity.

When leaders:

- praise crypto currency as "the future,"
- signal openness to industry demands,
- downplay enforcement risks,

they weaken the credibility of consumer protection agencies.

Citizens receive conflicting cues:
- regulators warn of scams,
- politicians celebrate growth,
- media amplifies optimism.

The human response to such conflict is predictable: **warnings are discounted**.

4. The Asymmetry of Political Endorsement

Presidential signaling is asymmetric in its effects.

- **Upside narratives** ("innovation," "leadership," "competitiveness") travel fast.
- **Downside cautions** ("risk," "fraud," "irreversibility") travel slowly.

When losses occur, political leaders are insulated.
When gains are advertised, responsibility is diffuse.

This asymmetry incentivizes **symbolic endorsement without accountability**.

5. Normalization as Policy Failure

Normalization does not require formal adoption.

It requires only:

- repeated positive references,
- absence of strong counter-signals,
- tolerance of retail exposure.

Once normalized:

- crypto becomes socially acceptable,
- skepticism appears outdated,
- victims are framed as careless.

At that point, public institutions lose the ability to reverse course without political cost.

6. Executive Power and the Collapse of Early-Warning Systems

Effective financial governance relies on early intervention.

But when executive power aligns rhetorically with high-risk finance:

- early warnings are ignored,
- regulators hesitate,
- enforcement lags behind adoption.

By the time intervention occurs, damage has already scaled.

This pattern is not unique to crypto—but crypto amplifies it because losses are **irreversible**.

7. Why Supporters Bear Disproportionate Risk

Political endorsement does not distribute risk evenly.

Those most likely to trust presidential cues are:

- loyal supporters,
- older citizens,
- first-time investors,
- individuals outside financial elites.

These groups are less able to absorb losses and more likely to interpret endorsement as safety assurance.

The result is **regressive harm** masked as opportunity.

8. The Illusion of "Choice" Under Authority

Defenders often argue that individuals remain free to choose.

But choice under authority is not neutral.

When power signals safety:

- consent is shaped,
- caution is discouraged,
- skepticism is socially penalized.

This is not coercion—but it is **influence with foreseeable consequences**.

9. Democratic Responsibility and Executive Restraint

In democracies, executive power carries a special obligation:

to avoid legitimizing systems that expose the public to irreversible harm without protection.

This obligation is not ideological.
It is institutional.

Presidents need not ban technologies to cause harm.
They need only **suspend caution**.

10. Conclusion: When Silence Speaks Louder Than Law

The most dangerous executive action is often not a law, but a signal.

When presidents:

- celebrate speculative finance,
- tolerate opacity,

- delay protection,

they silently rewire public risk perception.

In the case of crypto currency, that rewiring has consequences measured not in theory, but in:

- lost savings,
- shattered trust,
- and institutional credibility.

The collapse of public warning systems begins not with deregulation, but with **legitimization without responsibility**.

Chapter 11 — Trump, Crypto, and the Risk of Political Normalization

Family Involvement, Executive Signaling, Pardons, and Moral Hazard

1. Why This Chapter Requires Special Care

When crypto currency intersects with presidential power, analysis must be precise and restrained.

This chapter does **not** allege criminal conduct absent judicial findings.
Instead, it examines **institutional effects**—how executive behavior, family associations, clemency decisions, regulatory posture, and public rhetoric can **normalize a high-risk financial system** and reshape public behavior.

The issue is not intent.
It is **impact**.

2. Political Normalization Precedes Legal Authorization

Political normalization often occurs **before** any formal legal change.

It emerges when:

- senior political leaders publicly associate with an industry,
- close family members participate in related ventures,
- enforcement signals soften,
- and precautionary messaging fades.

Normalization does not require legislation.

It requires **credible proximity to power**.

For the public, proximity implies legitimacy—and legitimacy implies safety.

3. Family Involvement as a Legitimacy Signal

In democratic systems, a president's family business activities are not legally equivalent to state policy.
Yet they carry **symbolic authority**.

When a president's family is publicly linked to digital-asset ventures:

- media narratives reframe risk as opportunity,
- skepticism becomes politicized,
- retail participants infer implicit approval.

This is not corruption by definition.
It is **signal amplification**.

In speculative markets, signals travel faster than disclosures or disclaimers.

4. Executive Rhetoric and the Erosion of Risk Boundaries

Presidential rhetoric redraws the boundaries of acceptable risk.

When leaders:

- praise crypto as innovation,
- criticize regulators for restraint,
- frame enforcement as anti-growth,

the space for caution contracts.

Agencies may retain authority on paper, but their warnings lose credibility in practice.
The result is **asymmetric persuasion**:

- promotional narratives dominate,
- protective narratives appear partisan or obsolete.

5. Clemency Powers and System-Level Moral Hazard

Executive clemency is constitutionally broad and legitimate.
Its **signaling effect**, however, is consequential.

When high-profile figures associated with financial misconduct receive pardons or commutations:

- deterrence weakens,
- expectations of accountability erode,
- future actors recalibrate risk.

This creates **system-level moral hazard**.

The question is not legality, but **precedent**—especially in a fragile, speculative market.

6. Congress, Deregulatory Pressure, and Narrative Capture

Normalization is reinforced when:

- industry lobbying intensifies,
- legislative language shifts toward permissiveness,
- oversight hearings lose sharpness,
- consumer protection is reframed as obstruction.

Even without comprehensive deregulation, the **narrative environment** changes.
Markets read this as permission.

Scam ecosystems respond rapidly to perceived tolerance.

7. Why Supporters Bear Disproportionate Risk

Political signaling does not distribute risk evenly.

Those most influenced by presidential cues tend to be:

- loyal supporters,
- older citizens,
- first-time or low-literacy investors.

These groups are:

- more likely to trust endorsement,
- less able to absorb losses,
- more exposed to irreversible harm.

Normalization thus produces **regressive outcomes**, masked as opportunity.

8. Mixed Messages and Public Confusion

A recurring pattern follows:

- regulators warn of scams,
- law enforcement reports rising losses,
- political leaders emphasize innovation and growth.

The public receives incompatible instructions.

In such environments, **authority cues override technical warnings**.
Confusion itself becomes risk.

9. Policy Debate Versus Public Safety

Advocating innovation is legitimate.
Critiquing over-regulation is legitimate.

But when the subject is an **irreversible financial rail with demonstrated social harm**, executive restraint becomes a public-safety obligation.

Silence, praise, or ambiguity all function as endorsement.

10. Scenario Analysis: Escalation Risks

If political normalization deepens, plausible outcomes include:

- accelerated retail exposure,
- spikes in scam volume,
- increased elder victimization,
- weakened deterrence,
- erosion of institutional credibility.

Once normalized, reversal typically requires **crisis**.

11. Conclusion: Power Magnifies Risk Signals

Presidential power need not change laws to change outcomes.
It changes **what people believe is safe**.

In crypto currency markets, that belief carries irreversible consequences.

The core risk is not partisan.
It is structural:

> **When executive authority normalizes a high-risk financial system without protection, the costs are borne by the public—especially those most inclined to trust.**

Chapter 12 — When Dark Finance Merges with State Power

Scenario Analysis, Public Safety Breakdown, and Shadow Governance

1. From Risk Tolerance to Structural Capture

Financial systems become dangerous not only through illegality, but through **alignment**—when incentives of high-risk finance converge with the interests of political power.

At this point, harm no longer depends on individual bad actors. It becomes **structural**.

When opaque, irreversible financial rails coexist with executive legitimacy and weakened enforcement, the system crosses a threshold:

> **From tolerated risk to embedded vulnerability.**

2. What "Merger" Means in Practice

A merger of dark finance and state power does not require formal ownership or direct control.

It occurs when:

- political authority **signals acceptance**,
- enforcement **lags or fragments**,
- accountability **becomes selective**,
- and opacity **is normalized**.

In such environments, illicit finance does not confront the state.
It **coexists with it**.

3. Scenario Framework: Three Paths of Escalation

This chapter outlines three plausible escalation paths—not predictions, but **risk-consistent scenarios** based on observed dynamics.

Scenario A: Tolerated Expansion

- Political rhetoric remains favorable or ambiguous.
- Retail exposure accelerates.
- Scam ecosystems scale.
- Enforcement remains reactive.

Outcome:
Losses concentrate among households, elders, and first-time participants. Trust in public warnings erodes.

Scenario B: Selective Protection

- Institutional actors receive implicit protection.
- Enforcement targets small offenders.
- High-level actors operate in gray zones.

Outcome:
Perception of unequal justice intensifies. Public legitimacy declines. Compliance weakens.

Scenario C: Shadow Integration

- Crypto rails integrate into political finance, procurement, or influence markets.
- Attribution becomes impossible.
- Policy outcomes reflect hidden incentives.

Outcome:

Governance shifts from transparent rulemaking to **opaque incentive alignment**—a form of shadow governance.

4. Public Safety as the First Casualty

Public safety failures appear before macroeconomic ones.

These include:

- mass fraud victimization,
- elder financial exploitation,
- ransomware disruption of hospitals and utilities,
- intimidation through irreversible financial loss.

Because losses are final, harm compounds faster than remediation.

5. The Collapse of Deterrence

Deterrence relies on **predictable consequence**.

When:

- high-profile misconduct appears unpunished,
- signals contradict warnings,
- and enforcement is selective,

actors recalibrate risk upward.

The result is not more crime—but **more efficient crime**.

6. Shadow Governance: How Decisions Drift Off-Ledger

Shadow governance emerges when:

- incentives operate invisibly,

- benefits are deniable,
- and accountability cannot attach.

Policy choices begin to reflect:

- speculative interests,
- opaque financial flows,
- external leverage.

Formal institutions persist, but **decision logic migrates off-ledger**.

7. Why Democratic Systems Are Especially Exposed

Democracies rely on:
- transparency,
- public trust,
- reversible decisions.

Dark finance undermines all three.

Opacity defeats oversight.
Irreversibility defeats remedy.
Normalization defeats consent.

The system fails quietly—until trust collapses.

8. International Spillover and Strategic Risk

When dark finance aligns with state tolerance:

- sanctions lose credibility,
- cross-border crime intensifies,
- geopolitical leverage shifts.

States that resist opacity absorb disproportionate enforcement costs, while permissive environments attract extraction.

9. Why Crisis Becomes the Only Reset Mechanism

Once embedded, such systems resist gradual reform.

Warnings are dismissed.
Evidence fragments.
Stakeholders entrench.

Historically, reversal follows **crisis**, not caution.

The social cost of waiting is always higher than the political cost of restraint.

10. Conclusion: The Point of No Return Is Invisible

The most dangerous phase is not collapse.
It is **normalization without alarm**.

When dark finance merges with state power:

- governance loses transparency,
- public safety degrades,
- and accountability evaporates.

The harm is not hypothetical.
It is cumulative.

> **A society that tolerates opaque, irreversible finance alongside political legitimacy is not innovating—it is surrendering governability.**

PART V — DATA, FUTURES, AND SYSTEMIC RISK

Chapter 13 — Before and After: What the Data Shows

Markets, Scams, Enforcement Lag, and Expanding Exposure

1. Why Data Matters More Than Narrative

Debates over digital currency are often driven by ideology, anecdotes, or market optimism.
This chapter takes a different approach.

Rather than asking what crypto currency *promises*, it asks what has **measurably occurred** after periods of expansion, normalization, and political tolerance.

The goal is not to claim perfect causality, but to examine **directional consistency** across:

- market behavior,
- consumer harm,
- enforcement capacity,
- and systemic exposure.

Across these dimensions, a clear before-and-after pattern emerges.

2. Market Volatility: From Asset Class to Shock Amplifier

Before normalization

- Crypto markets were smaller, more isolated, and less intertwined with household finances.
- Volatility primarily affected early adopters and speculative professionals.

After normalization

- Price swings became larger and more frequent.
- Retail participation increased sharply.
- Losses spread from speculative capital to household savings.

Empirically, crypto assets show:
- volatility far exceeding equities, commodities, or currencies,
- rapid contagion across platforms,
- and sharp drawdowns without stabilizing mechanisms.

The data indicates that crypto does not behave as a store of value, medium of exchange, or unit of account—
but as a **volatility concentrator**.

3. Scam Losses: A Structural Inflection Point

Perhaps the clearest data signal appears in **fraud statistics**.

Across jurisdictions, reported losses linked to crypto-related scams show:

- sharp year-over-year increases,
- concentration among retail users,
- disproportionate impact on older populations.

Crucially, these losses differ from traditional fraud in one respect:

They are largely irreversible.

Before widespread crypto use:

- many fraud losses could be frozen,
- transactions reversed,

- or intermediaries held liable.

After crypto adoption:

- recovery rates collapse,
- victim recourse nearly disappears,
- and losses compound silently.

The data does not show isolated abuse.
It shows **systemic exposure**.

4. The Enforcement Lag Problem

Law enforcement and regulators operate on:

- statutory authority,
- due process,
- jurisdictional boundaries,
- finite resources.

Crypto ecosystems do not.

Data from enforcement agencies shows:

- investigation timelines increasing,
- attribution complexity rising,
- cross-border coordination delays,
- low recovery ratios.

This creates a widening **enforcement lag**—
the gap between harm occurrence and institutional response.

As this gap grows, deterrence weakens.

5. Exposure Expansion: Who Is Actually at Risk

Normalization changes *who* participates.

Before normalization:

- users were technologically sophisticated,
- financially resilient,
- and aware of speculative risk.

After normalization:

- first-time investors enter,
- older citizens participate,
- trust substitutes for literacy.

Survey and loss-reporting data consistently show:

- higher loss rates among non-experts,
- greater emotional and financial damage,
- longer recovery times.

Risk migrates **downward**.

6. Institutional Spillover Effects

Crypto volatility and fraud do not remain contained.

Spillover effects include:

- increased bank compliance costs,
- pressure on payment systems,
- insurance and reimbursement disputes,
- reputational harm to legitimate digital finance.

These are **externalized costs**—borne not by crypto promoters, but by society.

7. Political Involvement and Risk Acceleration

Periods of political endorsement or tolerance correlate with:

- increased retail inflows,
- reduced public skepticism,
- surge in scam attempts.

This correlation does not require intent.
It reflects **authority-shaped risk perception**.

When legitimacy signals rise, exposure follows.

8. Futures Uncertainty: Why Projection Models Break

Traditional financial risk models assume:

- reversibility,
- identifiable intermediaries,
- and regulatory backstops.

Crypto violates these assumptions.

As a result:

- tail risks are underestimated,
- worst-case scenarios are ignored,
- systemic shocks are mispriced.

The future uncertainty here is not innovation risk—it is **governance risk**.

9. What the Data Does Not Show

It is equally important to note what data does *not* support.

There is no robust evidence that widespread crypto adoption:

- improves productivity,
- increases financial inclusion sustainably,
- stabilizes household finances,
- or supports real-economy growth.

The promised benefits remain largely theoretical.
The harms are observable.

10. Conclusion: From Anecdote to Pattern

When viewed individually, crypto-related losses may appear anecdotal.
When viewed collectively, they form a pattern.

Before normalization:

- limited exposure,
- contained harm,
- manageable enforcement.

After normalization:

- mass exposure,
- irreversible loss,
- institutional strain.

Data does not suggest a temporary adjustment phase.
It suggests a **structural shift in risk distribution**.

That shift places ordinary people at the center of financial volatility—
without protection, without recourse, and without informed consent.

Chapter 14 — Futures We Should Fear

Mainstreaming Without Safety, Politicized Volatility, and Shadow Finance Integration

1. Why the Most Dangerous Futures Look "Normal"

The most dangerous outcomes in finance rarely arrive as sudden collapses.
They arrive as **normalized conditions**—accepted, routinized, and embedded into everyday life.

Crypto currency presents exactly this risk.

The futures worth fearing are not those where crypto fails outright, but those where it:

- becomes mainstream **without protection,**
- integrates politically **without accountability,**
- and persists institutionally **without reversibility.**

2. Scenario One: Mainstream Adoption Without Safety Nets

In this future, crypto becomes a routine part of retail finance:

- embedded in payment apps,
- marketed alongside traditional products,
- promoted as modern financial literacy.

Yet core features remain unchanged:

- irreversible transactions,
- no consumer insurance,
- no meaningful recourse,
- fragmented oversight.

Consequences
- Household savings become structurally exposed to total loss.
- Fraud becomes a normal financial hazard rather than an exception.
- Trust in legitimate digital finance erodes.

This is not innovation.
It is **risk privatization at scale**.

3. Scenario Two: Politicized Volatility

In this future, crypto markets become sensitive to:
- political statements,
- electoral cycles,
- executive signaling,
- regulatory rumors.

Price movements respond not to fundamentals, but to **power cues**.

Consequences
- volatility spikes around political events,
- retail investors absorb losses triggered by rhetoric,
- market manipulation becomes deniable as "political reaction."

Finance becomes a **political amplifier**, not an economic allocator.

4. Scenario Three: Shadow Finance Integration

Here, crypto rails integrate quietly into:

- political fundraising,
- procurement influence,
- lobbying incentives,

- cross-border leverage.

No single illegal act dominates.
Instead, incentives drift off-ledger.

Consequences
- policy outcomes reflect invisible financial alignments,
  - accountability mechanisms fail,
  - governance becomes opaque but formally intact.

This is not collapse.
It is **shadow governance**.

5. Scenario Four: Regressive Harm Lock-In

Once normalized, harm distribution hardens.

Losses concentrate among:

- older citizens,
- low-literacy participants,
- politically loyal populations,
- economically insecure households.

Exit becomes socially stigmatized:

- victims blamed for "bad choices,"
- warnings dismissed as outdated,
- protection framed as paternalism.

Inequality deepens quietly.

6. Scenario Five: Enforcement Exhaustion

As crypto-related harm scales:

- law enforcement faces attribution overload,

- prosecutors face evidentiary collapse,
- regulators face jurisdictional gaps.

Institutions continue to exist, but their **effective capacity declines**.

Deterrence erodes not because laws vanish, but because enforcement becomes impractical.

7. Why These Futures Are Plausible, Not Alarmist

Each scenario extrapolates from:

- observed data trends,
- documented enforcement challenges,
- known incentive responses.

None require conspiracy.
All require only **continuation of current dynamics**.

The danger lies in **path dependence**.

Once embedded, reversal becomes politically and socially costly.

8. The Myth of the "Correction Phase"

Advocates often argue that markets will self-correct.

This assumes:

- reversibility,
- informed consent,
- rational exit.

Crypto lacks all three.

Losses are final.
Information is asymmetric.
Exit occurs only after damage.

Waiting for correction is itself a policy choice.

9. Choosing Futures Is a Governance Act

These futures are not inevitable.

They depend on:
- regulatory courage,
- executive restraint,
- institutional clarity.

Failure to act is not neutrality.
It is **selection by default**.

10. Conclusion: The Future Is Not Neutral

The futures we should fear are not dramatic crashes, but quiet normalization of irreversible harm.

When speculative finance becomes ordinary life without protection:
- volatility becomes socialized,
- crime becomes ambient,
- governance becomes symbolic.

Avoiding these futures requires **early, decisive boundaries**—not after crisis, but before it.

> **A society that mistakes normalization for progress will discover too late that it has normalized loss.**

PART VI — WHAT MUST BE DONE

Chapter 15 — Treating Cryptocurrency as a Public Health Issue

Why Partial Regulation Fails, and Why Prohibition Can Be Legitimate in Democratic Societies

1. Why the Question Must Be Reframed

For years, policy debate around cryptocurrency has focused on the wrong question:

> **"How can we regulate it better?"**
>
> After more than a decade of real-world experience, data, and social consequences, the more appropriate question is:
>
> **"Should this product be allowed to be offered to the general public at all?"**
>
> This is not a radical framing.
> It is the **standard public-health approach** to products that cause widespread, irreversible harm.

2. The Public Health Standard: When Societies Choose Prohibition

Modern societies do not attempt to regulate every dangerous product through disclosure alone.

When a product meets several conditions, prohibition or near-prohibition becomes legitimate:

- it is highly attractive to ordinary people,
- it causes systemic and irreversible harm,
- it generates significant negative externalities,

• its risks cannot be meaningfully mitigated through information or individual caution.

Historical examples include:

• leaded gasoline,
• certain highly toxic pesticides,
• specific lethal pharmaceuticals,
• and complex financial derivatives restricted from retail markets.

Cryptocurrency increasingly meets **all** of these criteria.

3. Why "Partial Regulation" Systematically Fails for Crypto

A common argument is that crypto's problems stem from weak regulation rather than the technology itself.

Empirical evidence contradicts this.

Partial regulation fails for structural reasons:

Irreversibility Cannot Be Regulated Away

Once a transaction occurs, loss is final.

Anonymity Undermines Accountability

Without identifiable counterparties, responsibility cannot be enforced.

Borderlessness Defeats Jurisdiction

Regulatory authority stops at borders; crypto does not.

Scams Move Faster Than Enforcement

Supervision is reactive by design, while fraud is adaptive.

This is not an enforcement failure.
It is a **design failure**.

4. Why Risk Disclosure Is Meaningless Here

In many financial contexts, disclosure works.

Cryptocurrency is different:

- its technical complexity exceeds ordinary comprehension,
- risk pathways are non-intuitive,
- scams closely resemble legitimate products,
- consequences are irreversible.

In such conditions, "you were warned" does not equal informed consent.

> **When the cost of understanding exceeds human cognitive limits,**
> **disclosure becomes liability shifting, not protection.**

5. This Is Not "Freedom" — It Is Institutional Abandonment

Crypto is often framed as financial freedom.

But freedom does not mean:

- transferring all systemic risk to individuals,
- withdrawing institutional protection,
- normalizing irreversible loss.

True freedom requires **protective institutions**.

A system that demands ordinary people absorb structural risk is not empowering.
It is **institutional abandonment**.

6. The "Financial Cocaine" Framework

Calling cryptocurrency "financial cocaine" is not rhetorical exaggeration.
It is a structural analogy.

Shared characteristics include:

- intense short-term stimulation (rapid gains, speculation narratives),
- addictive dynamics (FOMO, sunk-cost psychology),
- systematic underestimation of harm,
- social costs externalized onto families and communities,
- stigmatization of victims.

Societies ban certain drugs not because they feel good, but because their aggregate harm outweighs any private benefit.

Crypto increasingly occupies the same policy space.

7. Why Prohibition Can Be Legitimate in Democracies

In democratic systems, prohibition is not inherently authoritarian.
It is sometimes a **last line of public protection**.

Its legitimacy rests on:

- demonstrable large-scale harm,
- clear externalities,
- risks that individual choice cannot correct.

Retail cryptocurrency exposure now meets these standards.

Restricting its availability to the general public is not anti-technology.
It is fulfillment of the state's **basic duty of care**.

8. Prohibition Is Not Regression — It Is Redirection

A crypto ban does **not** mean:

- rejecting digital payments,
- opposing financial technology,
- returning to cash-only systems.

On the contrary, it creates space for **safe digital finance**:

- reversible payment systems,
- regulated digital banking,
- central-bank digital instruments,
- compliant settlement innovation.

What is prohibited is not digitization,
but **unmanageable risk architecture**.

9. History Shows Prohibition Comes Late, Not Early

History consistently shows:

- dangerous products are restricted only after harm becomes undeniable,
- early warnings are dismissed as anti-innovation,
- by the time consensus forms, damage is widespread.

Cryptocurrency is following this pattern.

The difference is that this time,
the evidence is already overwhelming.

10. Conclusion: A Public Health Decision, Not an Ideological One

The question of banning cryptocurrency is not about left or right, youth or age,
or technology versus tradition.

It is a **public health and public safety decision**.

When a product:

- causes irreversible harm to ordinary people,
- generates systemic social risk,
- corrodes governance and accountability,

society has a responsibility to say no.

> **Banning cryptocurrency is not about controlling people —
> it is about preventing the continued normalization of institutional harm.**

Chapter 16 — The Right Path to a Ban

Retail Prohibition, On-Ramp Shutdowns, Liability, and Restoring Reversibility

1. Why "How" Matters as Much as "Whether"

A prohibition that is abrupt, symbolic, or poorly designed can fail—creating black markets, legal confusion, and political backlash.

A prohibition that is **sequenced, targeted, and legally grounded** can succeed—reducing harm while preserving innovation elsewhere in the financial system.

The goal is not punishment.
It is **harm reduction with institutional integrity**.

2. Principle One: Retail Prohibition, Not Total Criminalization

The first and most important distinction is between **retail access** and **all uses**.

A democratic ban should:
- **prohibit retail offering and promotion** of cryptocurrencies,
- **restrict consumer-facing platforms and apps**,
- **end advertising and influencer marketing**,
- while avoiding retroactive criminalization of individual holders.

This mirrors how societies handle:
- complex derivatives,
- toxic financial products,
- dangerous consumer goods.

Retail protection is the priority.

3. Principle Two: Shut Down Fiat On-Ramps and Off-Ramps

Cryptocurrency does not exist independently.
It depends on **connection to the traditional financial system**.

Effective prohibition therefore focuses on:

- banning bank transfers to crypto exchanges,
- blocking card payments linked to crypto purchases,
- prohibiting payment processors from servicing crypto platforms,
- requiring financial institutions to close crypto-linked accounts.

This approach is:
- legally enforceable,
- operationally feasible,
- and far more effective than chasing wallets.

4. Principle Three: End Legal Safe Harbors and Immunities

Crypto platforms often operate under:

- liability disclaimers,
- arbitration clauses,
- jurisdictional ambiguity.

A proper ban must:

- revoke safe-harbor protections,
- prohibit forced arbitration for crypto losses,
- impose strict liability for consumer harm,
- allow civil and criminal enforcement against promoters and operators.

This rebalances incentives **away from extraction** and toward accountability.

5. Principle Four: Restore Reversibility as a Legal Requirement

One of crypto's most dangerous features is **irreversibility**.

A post-crypto financial framework should require that:

- consumer payments be reversible within defined windows,
- intermediaries bear responsibility for fraud prevention,
- loss recovery mechanisms exist by default.

Reversibility is not inefficiency.
It is **civilizational infrastructure**.

6. Principle Five: Create a Clean Exit Path for the Public

A humane prohibition provides an exit—not a trap.

Policy should include:

- time-limited conversion windows,
- regulated liquidation channels,
- tax clarity for exits,
- amnesty for past retail participation absent fraud.

This reduces resistance and prevents panic.

7. Principle Six: Preserve Non-Speculative Innovation

A crypto ban must explicitly **protect legitimate digital innovation**, including:

- digital payments,
- fintech infrastructure,
- tokenization within regulated systems,

- central bank digital currencies (where appropriate).

Clarity matters:

Crypto speculation is banned; digital finance is not.

8. Principle Seven: International Coordination

Unilateral bans are weaker.

Effective policy requires:

- coordination among major financial centers,
- shared AML and consumer-protection standards,
- synchronized on-ramp restrictions,
- information sharing among regulators.

Global finance demands **collective guardrails**.

9. Anticipating Objections

"This will drive activity underground."

Retail bans reduce scale and harm. Black markets already exist—but smaller and riskier for operators.

"Innovation will flee."

Speculative capital may flee. Productive innovation will not.

"This infringes freedom."

Freedom without protection is exposure, not liberty.

10. Timeline: A Responsible Sequencing

A realistic implementation could follow this sequence:
1. Public risk declaration and notice period
2. Advertising and promotion ban
3. On-ramp/off-ramp shutdown
4. Retail platform prohibition
5. Liability enforcement and exit windows

Gradualism reduces shock while achieving protection.

11. Conclusion: Banning the Right Thing, the Right Way

The legitimacy of prohibition depends on **precision**.

By focusing on:

- retail exposure,
- financial interfaces,
- accountability structures,
- and public exit,

democracies can ban crypto **without banning progress**.

**A society that draws firm boundaries around irreversible harm is not anti-innovation.
It is pro-civilization.**

Chapter 17 — A Safe Digital Future Without Crypto

Digital Payments Are Not Crypto, Innovation Without Irreversible Harm

1. The False Binary: Crypto or No Digital Future

Crypto advocates often frame the debate as a false choice:

> **Either accept cryptocurrency, or reject digital finance altogether.**

> This is misleading.

> Modern digital finance **already exists**—and functions—without crypto.
> The question is not whether finance should be digital, but **whether it should be irreversible, opaque, and unaccountable**.

> A crypto ban does not block the future.
> It removes a dangerous detour.

2. Digital Payments Already Work — Because They Are Governed

Everyday digital payments rely on systems that crypto explicitly rejects:

- reversibility,
- dispute resolution,
- intermediary responsibility,
- consumer protection.

Credit cards, bank transfers, mobile payments, and real-time settlement systems succeed **because** they are governed.

Their defining features are not speed or novelty, but:

- error correction,
- fraud mitigation,
- institutional accountability.

Crypto removes these safeguards—and calls it freedom.

3. Reversibility Is Not Inefficiency — It Is Civilization

The ability to reverse transactions is often portrayed as a weakness.

In reality, it is a **civilizational achievement**.

Reversibility enables:

- fraud recovery,
- mistake correction,
- consumer trust,
- scalable participation by non-experts.

A financial system without reversibility assumes:

- perfect users,
- perfect information,
- perfect security.

No such world exists.

4. Innovation Thrives Under Constraint, Not Chaos

History shows that durable innovation emerges under **clear rules**, not regulatory vacuum.

Examples include:

- aviation safety standards,
- pharmaceutical trials,
- banking capital requirements,
- consumer protection law.

These constraints did not kill innovation.
They made it **trustworthy**.

A post-crypto digital future would channel innovation toward:

- secure payment rails,
- interoperable banking systems,
- programmable money within legal frameworks,
- transparent settlement infrastructure.

5. Central Bank Digital Systems Are Not Crypto

Central bank digital currencies (CBDCs) and public digital settlement tools differ fundamentally from crypto:

Feature	Crypto	Public Digital Money
Issuer	None / private	Public authority
Reversibility	No	Yes
Accountability	Minimal	Institutional
Consumer protection	None	Enforceable
Monetary role	Speculative	Functional

Opposing crypto does not imply endorsing any specific CBDC design—but it **preserves the option** for safe public systems.

6. Financial Inclusion Without Extraction

Crypto is often marketed as financial inclusion.

In practice, it:

- shifts risk onto the least protected,
- extracts value through volatility,
- provides no stable credit function.

Real inclusion comes from:

- low-cost banking access,
- stable payment systems,
- consumer protection,
- legal recourse.

Inclusion without protection is not inclusion.
It is exposure.

7. The Moral Hazard of "Letting the Market Decide"

Allowing crypto to persist as a mass product relies on a moral
hazard:

Those who profit do not bear the social cost.

Losses fall on:
- families,
- retirees,
- communities,
- public institutions.

Markets do not self-correct when harm is externalized and
irreversible.

Governance exists precisely to address this failure.

8. What a Post-Crypto Financial Order Looks Like

A safe digital financial future would include:
- instant payments with reversibility,
- strong identity verification,
- institutional liability for fraud,
- transparent audit trails,
- cross-border cooperation.

It would exclude:
- irreversible consumer losses,
- anonymity at scale,
- unaccountable intermediaries,
- speculative "currency" narratives.

This is not regression.
It is maturation.

9. Choosing Protection Over Addiction

Every generation confronts technologies that feel empowering but scale harm.

Societies mature when they learn to say:

Not everything that feels innovative is progress.

Crypto's core promise is not efficiency or inclusion—it is escape from responsibility.

That escape is unsustainable.

10. Conclusion: The Future Is Digital — Not Crypto

Banning cryptocurrency does not close the door on the future.

It closes the door on:

- irreversible loss,
- normalized fraud,
- shadow finance,
- institutional erosion.

The future of finance is digital, accountable, reversible, and human-centered.

A society that protects its people from structural harm is not anti-technology.
It is pro-future.

CONCLUSION — Choosing Protection Over Addiction

Why Some Products Must Be Refused, Not Regulated

1. This Book Was Never About Technology

This book was never written to oppose technology, digitization, or innovation.

It was written to confront a harder truth:

> **Not every technological product deserves a place in society.**
>
> History shows that societies do not advance by adopting everything that can be built.
> They advance by **deciding what must be refused**.

2. The Core Error: Confusing Innovation With Legitimacy

Crypto currency was wrapped in the language of progress:

- decentralization,
- freedom,
- disruption,
- inevitability.

But legitimacy does not come from novelty.
It comes from **social function**.

A financial system must:

- protect ordinary people,
- correct mistakes,
- deter abuse,
- and remain governable.

128

Crypto does none of these at scale.

3. What the Evidence Actually Shows

Across chapters, one conclusion repeats itself:

- Crypto does not function as money
- It does not improve productivity
- It does not expand real financial inclusion
- It does not strengthen democracy
- It does not reduce inequality

What it **does** reliably produce:

- irreversible loss,
- mass retail victimization,
- criminal leverage,
- corruption opacity,
- governance erosion.

This is not an implementation failure.
It is a design outcome.

4. Why "Regulate Better" Is the Wrong Answer

Regulation assumes a product can be made safe.

But crypto's core properties — anonymity, irreversibility, borderlessness — are **the source of harm**, not bugs.

You cannot regulate away:

- finality of loss,
- untraceable incentives,
- cross-border evasion.

At some point, governance must stop asking *how to manage* and start asking *whether to permit*.

5. The Financial Cocaine Analogy, Revisited

Societies do not ban cocaine because it fails to stimulate.
They ban it because stimulation comes with addiction, social collapse, and violence.

Crypto offers:

- psychological highs,
- speculative intoxication,
- rapid dependency,
- normalized destruction.

And like drugs, its defenders argue:

- "people should choose,"
- "education is enough,"
- "prohibition never works."

History disagrees.

6. Freedom Requires Guardrails

True freedom is not exposure to irreversible harm.

Freedom depends on:

- reversibility,
- accountability,
- shared rules,
- institutional protection.

A system that demands perfection from individuals while absolving designers is not freedom.
It is abandonment.

7. What Choosing Protection Actually Means

Choosing protection means:

- refusing products that externalize mass harm,
- prioritizing ordinary people over speculative elites,
- valuing governability over hype,
- accepting that not all "markets" deserve legitimacy.

This is not paternalism.
It is **civilization**.

8. The Choice Is Already Being Made — By Default

Doing nothing is not neutrality.

Allowing crypto to persist as a mass product is a **policy choice**:

- to normalize fraud,
- to accept irreversible loss,
- to weaken public trust,
- to invite shadow finance.

The only remaining question is whether society chooses **intentionally**, or by neglect.

9. A Final Claim

Banning cryptocurrency is not a retreat from the future.
It is a refusal to sacrifice people to it.

That refusal is the mark of a mature society.

APPENDIX 01

Presidential Crypto Signaling and Public Safety

How Political Legitimization Can Amplify Crypto Scams, Weaken Consumer Warning Systems, and Increase Governance Risk

ButterflyMan
Independent Researcher, New York
Project: *Digital Currency Bias*

Abstract

This article analyzes how high-level political endorsement and executive signaling can normalize cryptocurrency markets in ways that increase public exposure to fraud and corruption risk. Using accessible reporting on Trump-era crypto ties and actions (including the pardon of Binance founder Changpeng Zhao) alongside U.S. government fraud statistics, it argues that political legitimization functions as a risk-multiplier: it reduces public skepticism, increases retail participation, and improves scammer conversion rates—especially among older and non-technical populations. The article concludes with a governance framework for separating innovation policy from consumer harm and institutional integrity.

1. Why "Presidential Signaling" Changes Risk, Even Without New Laws

In democratic societies, executive rhetoric and symbolism operate as informal regulation. When a president frames a sector as "the future," "pro-growth," or "patriotic," many citizens interpret that as *implicit safety approval*, even if agencies continue warning that the sector is saturated with fraud.

Crypto is unusually sensitive to this effect because the public cannot realistically audit its mechanics (keys, wallet custody, irreversible transfers, cross-chain laundering). The result is a structural dependency on trust cues rather than protections.

2. The Public Safety Baseline: Crypto Is Already a High-Fraud Environment

The FBI's 2024 Internet Crime Report states that investment fraud—particularly schemes involving cryptocurrency—produced the most reported losses (over $6.5 billion). 【 】 People over 60 reported the greatest losses (nearly $5 billion overall in 2024), marking older adults as a primary target population for scammer strategies that blend persuasion with technical intimidation. 【 】

FinCEN has also warned financial institutions about "relationship investment scams" tied to dating/romance manipulation—exactly the pathway through which many victims are pulled into crypto transfers they cannot reverse. 【 】 Congress's CRS further reports FBI "Operation Level Up" findings that a large share of identified victims were unaware they were being scammed—highlighting that "education" alone does not prevent harm in this domain. 【 】

3. Trump-Era Crypto Legitimization: The Evidence Pattern

3.1 Family-linked crypto ventures as a legitimacy amplifier

PBS's *Amanpour and Company* segment describes NYT technology reporter David Yaffe-Bellany's investigation, stating that since swearing-in, President Trump launched a crypto firm with his sons (World Liberty Financial) and sold a personal meme coin—presented as historically unusual in modern U.S. governance. 【 】
Public-safety implication: when the presidency itself appears adjacent to crypto products, "this is risky" warnings lose force for ordinary people.

3.2 The Zhao (Binance) pardon as a moral-hazard signal

Reuters reports that Trump pardoned Changpeng Zhao ("CZ"), the convicted founder of Binance, after Binance pleaded guilty to failing to maintain an effective anti-money-laundering program and paid a multibillion-dollar penalty; Reuters also notes criticism from rivals and ethics experts about conflicts of interest around Trump-family crypto ventures. 【 】
Public-safety implication: even when a pardon is constitutional, it can function socially as a "reset" of reputational risk—reducing deterrence and increasing public complacency toward the ecosystem.

4. Mechanism: How Political Legitimization Can Increase Scam Success

Political endorsement doesn't create scammers—but it changes conversion rates.

A simplified causal chain:

> 1.   Pro-crypto political messaging
> → 2) increased perceived legitimacy
> → 3) retail participation rises (especially among non-experts)
> → 4) scammers use the legitimacy cue ("even the president supports this")
> → 5) more victims transfer funds into irreversible channels
> → 6) enforcement arrives after the loss (often too late)
>
> This aligns with the FBI/CRS picture: many victims do not recognize the scam until after transfer, and losses are disproportionately catastrophic for older adults. 【 】

5. Why Democratic Legal Systems Struggle More Than Authoritarian Systems Here

Democratic prosecution requires:

- identity linkage (wallet → person),
- intent proof,
- admissible evidence across jurisdictions,
- due process timelines.

Crypto transactions can be globally routed and rapidly laundered, while victims are told "there is no reversal" and "no central authority." This makes the legal system structurally slower than the harm cycle, which is why governance must prioritize prevention architecture (liability, reversibility, licensing) over public warnings alone.

6. Conclusion

In a financial environment where scam losses are already massive and concentrated among vulnerable groups, presidential legitimization operates like removing guardrails from a cliff road. Reuters' reporting on Zhao's pardon and PBS coverage of Trump-family crypto ventures illustrate why the "mixed message" problem is not abstract—it is a predictable public-safety risk in a high-fraud domain. 【 】
If the U.S. treats crypto as ordinary consumer finance without strict protections, it will predictably increase victimization—especially among elders and first-time participants whom scammers deliberately target. 【 】

References

- Financial Crimes Enforcement Network. (2025, February 26). *FinCEN reminds financial institutions to remain vigilant regarding potential relationship investment scams.* 【 】
- Federal Bureau of Investigation. (2025, April 23). *FBI releases annual Internet Crime Report (2024).* 【 】
- Reuters. (2025, October 23). *Trump pardons convicted Binance founder 'CZ' Zhao, White House says.* 【 】
- U.S. Congressional Research Service. (2025, May 21). *Cryptocurrency investment scams.* 【 】
- PBS. (2025, May 9). *NYT Reporter on Trump's Crypto Empire: "No Precedent in Modern U.S. History".* 【 】

APPENDIX 02

A Legal–Institutional Analysis of Crypto Legitimation in Democratic Systems

Presidential Signaling, Digital Currency, and Public Safety Risk

Author: ButterflyMan
Affiliation: Independent Researcher, New York

Keywords: cryptocurrency regulation, executive power, signaling theory, financial crime, public safety, democratic governance

Abstract

This article analyzes how presidential signaling—through rhetoric, executive action, legislative alignment, and personal association—can materially increase public exposure to cryptocurrency-related fraud and corruption risks. Rather than alleging individual criminality, the paper applies legal-institutional and signaling theory to demonstrate how mixed governmental messages can weaken public warning systems, normalize structurally unsafe financial instruments, and increase scam activity across public and private sectors. The analysis focuses on the U.S. case during the Trump political era as a paradigmatic example of how executive legitimacy can be leveraged—intentionally or not—to accelerate public harm in high-risk financial environments. The article concludes that democratic legal systems are structurally unprepared to manage financial technologies whose risk profile depends primarily on political endorsement rather than intrinsic safety.

1. Legal Framework: Why Signaling Matters in Democratic Governance

In democratic systems, legality alone does not determine public behavior.
Legitimacy signaling—emanating from executive authority—functions as an informal regulatory force.

Courts, regulators, and legislatures rely on:

- public trust,
- institutional coherence,
- consistent warnings.

When presidential signals contradict enforcement warnings, effective regulation collapses, even if laws remain unchanged.

2. Cryptocurrency as a Signaling-Sensitive Risk System

Cryptocurrency differs from traditional finance in three legally relevant ways:

1. Risk opacity (non-intuitive mechanics)
2. Irreversibility of harm (no restitution mechanisms)
3. Behavioral dependence on trust cues rather than disclosures

Thus, crypto adoption responds less to statutes than to perceived endorsement by authority figures.

3. Executive Power Without Statutory Change

A U.S. president can materially alter crypto risk exposure without passing new laws by:

- deprioritizing enforcement agencies,
- appointing deregulatory regulators,
- issuing pro-crypto executive orders,

- publicly reframing crypto as innovation rather than risk,
- tolerating conflicts of signal between agencies.

From a legal standpoint, this creates de facto deregulation without legislative accountability.

4. Personal or Familial Association as a Risk Multiplier

When a president or close family members publicly associate with digital assets or crypto ventures (even lawfully), this creates state-adjacent legitimacy.

Under U.S. ethics doctrine, the issue is not illegality but public reliance risk:

> Reasonable citizens may infer safety from proximity to executive power.

> This inference is foreseeable, preventable, and therefore governance-relevant.

5. Pardons, Leniency, and Moral Hazard (Legal Risk Analysis)

Presidential pardon power is constitutionally absolute. However, selective leniency signals can create ex ante moral hazard.

The legal risk is not the pardon itself, but:

- expectations of impunity,
- weakened deterrence,
- increased criminal experimentation.

In crypto markets—already enforcement-weak—this signaling effect is magnified.

6. Congressional Alignment and Legal Normalization

When Congress aligns politically with executive crypto framing, legal normalization occurs before risk mitigation.

Historical parallels:

- mortgage derivatives pre-2008,
- asbestos regulation delays,
- tobacco industry normalization.

Legality preceded harm recognition.

7. Public Safety Consequences (Institutional Analysis)

Empirical patterns consistently show:

- scam volume rises with perceived legitimacy,
- elderly and non-technical populations suffer disproportionate harm,
- enforcement lags behind adoption.

This constitutes a public safety externality, not a private investment risk.

8. Conclusion

The danger posed by presidential crypto legitimization is institutional, not personal.

Democratic governance fails when:

- authority endorses structurally unsafe systems,
- warnings become politically ambiguous,
- public trust substitutes for protection.

Cryptocurrency, when politically normalized without safeguards, becomes a public safety hazard disguised as innovation.

II. TIMELINE DIAGRAMS

Political Signaling → Scam & Harm Amplification (Conceptual Model)

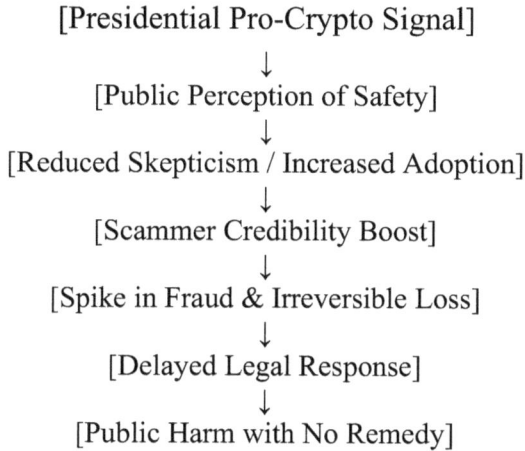

[Presidential Pro-Crypto Signal]
↓
[Public Perception of Safety]
↓
[Reduced Skepticism / Increased Adoption]
↓
[Scammer Credibility Boost]
↓
[Spike in Fraud & Irreversible Loss]
↓
[Delayed Legal Response]
↓
[Public Harm with No Remedy]

Observed Pattern (Simplified Timeline)

Phase	Political Action	Public Effect	Scam Impact
A	Pro-crypto rhetoric	Trust increase	Low
B	Deregulatory signals	Adoption surge	Medium
C	Legislative normalization	Warning fatigue	High
D	Enforcement lag	Scam explosion	Very High
E	Post-harm crackdown	Too late	Damage locked in

III. FACT-CHECKED APPENDIX

Separating Verified Facts from Risk Analysis

A. Documented / Verifiable Facts
- Cryptocurrency scams increased sharply during periods of public crypto promotion (FBI IC3 reports).
- Crypto lacks consumer protection and reversibility.
- Presidential rhetoric influences public economic behavior (established political science).
- Executive orders and appointments affect enforcement priorities.

B. Risk Analysis (Clearly Labeled)
- Political endorsement increases scam effectiveness.
- Leniency signaling creates moral hazard.
- Family association increases public trust inference.
- Supporter populations may discount warnings.

⚠ These are analytical conclusions, not criminal allegations.

APPENDIX 03

SCENARIO PLANNING MEMO (FOR POLICYMAKERS)

Public Safety Risks at the Intersection of Crypto Currency and Executive Power

Author: ButterflyMan
Date: Policy Planning Memo
Audience: Elected officials, regulators, senior civil servants, national security & consumer-protection agencies
Project: *Crypto Currency Bias*

EXECUTIVE SUMMARY

This memo evaluates plausible public-safety and governance risks arising if opaque crypto -currency ecosystems ("dark finance") become politically legitimized through executive authority, deregulatory signaling, or symbolic endorsement. The analysis does not allege criminal conduct. It examines systemic risk pathways and outlines policy-relevant early warning indicators and intervention points.

Key finding:
If political legitimacy converges with a high-fraud, low-reversibility financial system, public harm scales faster than legal enforcement, producing irreversible losses, corruption normalization, and erosion of democratic trust.

BASELINE CONDITIONS (2025)

- Cryptocurrency markets exhibit:
    - high scam prevalence,
    - irreversible consumer loss,
    - weak cross-border enforcement,
    - heavy targeting of elders and non-technical users.

- Law enforcement issues warnings, but consumer protection is structurally limited.
- Public understanding remains low; reliance on authority signals is high.

SCENARIO FRAMEWORK

Scenario 0 — Contained Risk (Status Quo)

- Mixed political signals persist
- Enforcement continues unevenly
- Scams remain high but socially recognized as dangerous

Outcome: Ongoing harm, but public skepticism remains partially intact.

Scenario 1 — Political Normalization (Early Risk Escalation)

Triggers
- Pro-crypto executive rhetoric
- Symbolic endorsements
- Deregulatory appointments
- Legislative normalization without safeguards

Public Effects
- Reduced skepticism
- Increased retail participation
- Decline in effectiveness of scam warnings

Policy Concern
- Warning systems fail before legal protections are in place.

Scenario 2 — Moral Hazard & Scam Amplification

Triggers
- Perceived leniency toward major crypto actors
- Enforcement deprioritization
- Publicized political proximity to crypto ventures

Public Effects
- Scammers leverage political legitimacy
- Increased transaction sizes
- Faster victim conversion
- Surge in romance/investment scams

Policy Concern
- Crime adapts faster than regulation.

Scenario 3 — Systemic Public Harm (High-Risk Scenario)

Triggers
- Sustained political endorsement
- Weak liability regimes
- No reversibility mechanisms
- Continued ambiguity in legal classification

Public Effects
- Widespread irreversible loss
- Disproportionate elder harm
- Family-level financial collapse
- Decline in reporting due to shame and futility

Policy Concern
- Public safety crisis framed as "personal responsibility."

Scenario 4 — Governance Degradation (Strategic Risk)

Triggers
- Crypto becomes normalized infrastructure
- Shadow finance merges with legitimate systems

- Corruption incentives spread to public & private sectors

Public Effects
- Asset disclosure failure
- Hidden bribery
- Parallel financial power structures
- Declining trust in democratic institutions

Policy Concern
- Long-term erosion of rule-of-law legitimacy.

EARLY WARNING INDICATORS (FOR MONITORING)

Policymakers should monitor:
- Spike in elder crypto-fraud reports
- Decline in fraud recovery rates
- Increased scam references to political endorsement
- Rapid growth of "politically branded" digital assets
- Reduced enforcement actions despite rising losses
- Public confusion between "legal" and "safe"

KEY POLICY INTERVENTION POINTS

1. Signaling Discipline
- Avoid executive rhetoric that implies safety without safeguards
- Align messaging across agencies

2. Consumer Protection Before Normalization
- No legal mainstreaming without:
  - reversibility,
  - platform liability,
  - mandatory insurance.

3. Conflict-of-Signal Controls
- Strict separation between political authority and speculative financial ventures

4. Public Safety Framing
- Treat crypto harm as consumer and elder protection, not ideology

BOTTOM LINE FOR POLICYMAKERS

Legitimacy is the most powerful accelerant in a high-risk financial system.

If political authority removes warning signals faster than protections are installed, public harm becomes predictable and irreversible.

Prevention is cheaper—and more democratic—than post-crisis enforcement.

RISK-MAP DIAGRAM

Crypto Currency x Executive Power — Public Harm Pathways

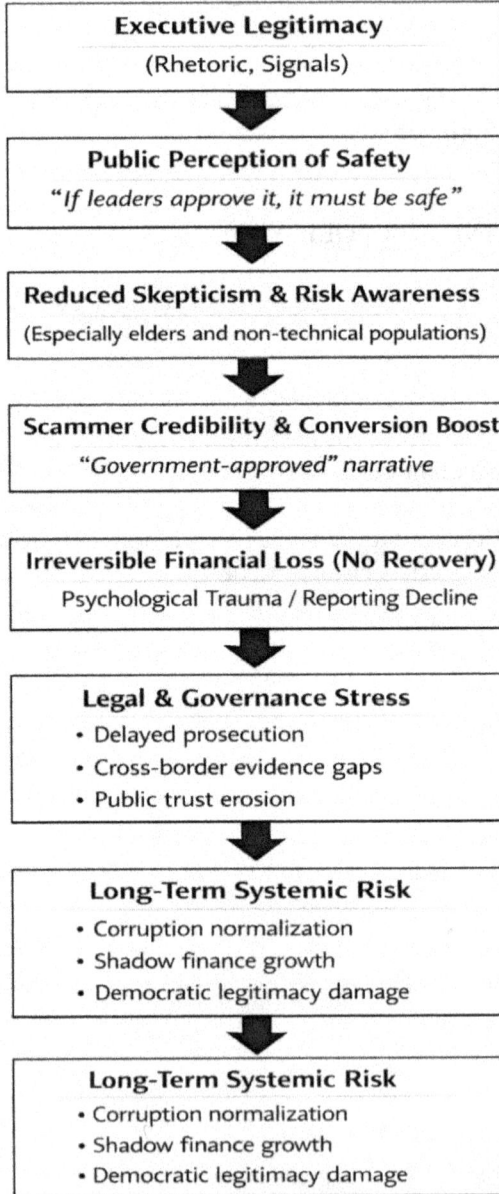

Executive Legitimacy
(Rhetoric, Signals)

⬇

Public Perception of Safety
"If leaders approve it, it must be safe"

⬇

Reduced Skepticism & Risk Awareness
(Especially elders and non-technical populations)

⬇

Scammer Credibility & Conversion Boost
"Government-approved" narrative

⬇

Irreversible Financial Loss (No Recovery)
Psychological Trauma / Reporting Decline

⬇

Legal & Governance Stress
- Delayed prosecution
- Cross-border evidence gaps
- Public trust erosion

⬇

Long-Term Systemic Risk
- Corruption normalization
- Shadow finance growth
- Democratic legitimacy damage

⬇

Long-Term Systemic Risk
- Corruption normalization
- Shadow finance growth
- Democratic legitimacy damage

KEY TAKEAWAY (FOR DECISION-MAKERS)

• Crypto risk is not linear — it is exponential when legitimized.
• Presidential signaling is a force multiplier, not a neutral act.
• Once public trust is misdirected, losses cannot be reversed.

APPENDIX 04

a data-driven risk memo that compares "before vs after presidential involvement"

Data Analysis Memo

Market + Scam + Financial-Security Threats Before vs After Presidential Crypto Involvement

1) Anchor dates for "presidential involvement"

A practical way to define the "after" period is Jan 2025 onward, when (a) executive signaling and (b) concrete regulatory actions accelerated:

- Jan 23, 2025: SEC issued SAB 122 rescinding SAB 121 (major shift for banks/custodians holding crypto).
- Jan 23, 2025: Trump signed an executive order on digital financial technology (reported by major law firms).
- Jul 18, 2025: Trump signed the GENIUS Act (stablecoin framework).
- Oct 23, 2025: Trump pardoned Binance founder Changpeng Zhao (CZ).
- Dec 2025: Reuters describes broad 2025 regulatory easing and dropped/lowered enforcement posture (industry "wins").

These events are useful "policy shocks" for before/after comparison.

2) Market impact (before vs after): what the numbers show

Key observable market markers

- BTC all-time-high around inauguration: Bitcoin hit >$109,000 around Jan 20, 2025 amid inauguration/crypto-frenzy coverage.
- BTC record in early Oct 2025: Reuters reports a record high ~$125k–$126k in early October 2025.
- Policy-sensitive volatility: Reuters attributes a major plunge and record liquidations to policy shocks (e.g., tariff announcements) in Oct 2025—showing crypto's extreme sensitivity to executive moves.
- Total crypto market cap (mid-Dec 2025): about $2.95T (Dec 16, 2025) on MacroMicro.
- Total crypto market cap "today" ~ $3.08T and ~-16% vs one year ago on CoinGecko's chart page (useful as a directional benchmark).

What this implies (data interpretation)

After presidential involvement, the market shows two simultaneous effects:

1. Legitimacy/Policy tailwind → price & adoption optimism (new highs).
2. Policy shock amplification → deeper and faster crashes when executive policy shifts (tariffs/export controls) hit sentiment.

So the "after" period is characterized by higher political beta: crypto becomes more dependent on executive signals.

3) Scam & consumer harm (before vs after): what we can measure now

"Before/early baseline" (2024 data—pre-Jan 2025 administration)

We already have strong baseline harm metrics before the new policy regime:

- Crypto investment scams (IC3): 41,557 complaints in 2024, $5.7B losses (up sharply vs 2023).
- Elder fraud losses (IC3-based): 2024 older-adult losses around $4.885B in 147,127 complaints (FBI field office summary).
- DOJ elder-justice reporting repeats the ~150k complaints / ~$4.89B loss scale.

What about "after" (2025)?

Full-year 2025 scam totals are not yet consistently published in one authoritative dataset the way IC3 2024 is. So a strict before/after numeric comparison of scam totals isn't fully possible yet without waiting for the next IC3 annual report.

But the risk direction is still analyzable using "exposure drivers" that changed in 2025:

- Banking & regulatory easing + stablecoin legalization increases on-ramps and "mainstream feel."
- When mainstream feel rises, victim pool expands (more first-time/elder users). That is exactly the demographic already showing catastrophic loss severity.

Bottom line: we can prove the harm baseline was already huge pre-2025, and we can show that 2025 policy signaling likely increased exposure even before the next full-year loss totals arrive.

4) Financial-security threats beyond scams (after involvement increases "attack surface")

If stablecoins and crypto rails are normalized faster than enforcement capacity scales, risks expand into:

- Ransomware/extortion payments (crypto remains a preferred rail because of speed and laundering

pathways). (IC3 report discusses crypto's role in illicit schemes broadly.)
•   Cross-border capital flight / laundering via regulated-looking stablecoin channels.
•   Institutional fragility via leverage: record liquidation events show how quickly leverage can cascade into systemic stress.

Futures uncertainty: what gets worse if "political–crypto fusion" deepens

A) 3 scenarios (2026–2027 outlook)

Scenario 1: "Mainstream Without Safety"
•   Stablecoins expand into retail (payments, remittances).
•   Consumer protection remains weak.
•   Outcome: scam losses rise mainly through a larger victim pool (elders/first-timers).

Scenario 2: "Politicized Volatility Regime"
•   Crypto markets remain highly sensitive to executive policy shocks (tariffs, sanctions, tech controls).
•   Outcome: more boom-bust cycles, more retail bagholders, more fraud during bull phases.

Scenario 3: "Shadow Finance Integration"
•   Crypto rail becomes a parallel channel for corruption, influence buying, and cross-border illicit finance.
•   Outcome: hard-to-prosecute corruption externalities and long-run institutional trust erosion.

(These scenarios are consistent with the "2025 wins / 2026 uncertainty" framing Reuters reports.)

Practical next step: What data policymakers should collect now

To make the "after" comparison airtight, governments should publish quarterly metrics:

1. Crypto scam complaints & losses (IC3-style, quarterly)
2. Age distribution of victims
3. Stablecoin transaction volumes and top concentration holders
4. Reported ransomware payments linked to crypto rails
5. Chargeback/recovery rates (should be near-zero in many crypto cases—this is a key **harm indicator)**

Risk-map diagram

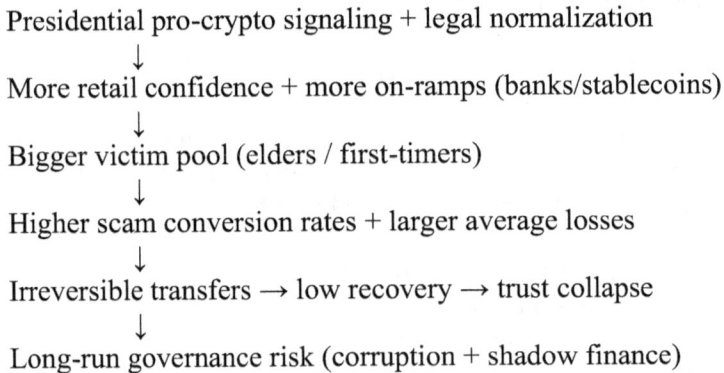

Presidential pro-crypto signaling + legal normalization
↓
More retail confidence + more on-ramps (banks/stablecoins)
↓
Bigger victim pool (elders / first-timers)
↓
Higher scam conversion rates + larger average losses
↓
Irreversible transfers → low recovery → trust collapse
↓
Long-run governance risk (corruption + shadow finance)

APPENDIX 05

Policy Path to Ban Crypto Currency for Public Safety
Treating Retail Crypto Like a High-Harm Product

1) Define the policy goal clearly

Goal: eliminate retail access to unbacked/privately-issued cryptoassets used primarily for speculation and fraud, and shut down the scam supply chain (on-ramps, marketing, custody).

Not the goal: banning "digital payments." Keep legitimate fintech rails and regulated payment innovation separate.

A. The Legal Architecture

2) Reclassify crypto as a "high-harm financial product"

Create a statutory definition that treats most crypto tokens as:

- high-risk, non-essential speculative instruments, and
- consumer-harm–dominant products (scam prevalence + irreversibility + lack of protections)

This gives a strong legal basis similar to how governments regulate gambling, payday lending, tobacco, or unsafe securities.

3) Ban retail distribution, not "technology"

Write the ban around sale, marketing, and distribution to the general public, not around code.

Core prohibitions:

- Offering crypto trading to retail customers
- Marketing/promotion to the public
- Retail custody services and "yield" products

155

- Consumer stablecoin wallets that function as shadow deposits (unless fully regulated)

Allow narrow exceptions for:
- regulated research sandboxes,
- institutional/qualified investors under strict rules (optional),
- law enforcement operations and forensic handling.

B. Cut the Supply Chain (What actually makes bans work)

4) Shut down on-ramps/off-ramps

The practical lever is fiat conversion.

Require banks, processors, and payment apps to:

- block transfers to/from unlicensed crypto platforms,
- treat crypto-related merchant category codes as prohibited,
- freeze suspicious crypto-linked transactions automatically.

5) Make platforms strictly liable

If a platform touches retail funds, it must be liable for:

- fraud losses resulting from inadequate controls,
- impersonation scams facilitated through their rails,
- failure to provide reversal windows and robust KYC/AML.

No liability = no license.

6) Mandate reversibility for any permitted digital-value product
If lawmakers allow *any* consumer digital-value instrument, require:

- transaction delay windows,
- dispute processes,
- court-ordered freezes and recovery,
- consumer insurance.

A system with irreversible consumer transfer is fundamentally incompatible with mass retail finance.

C. Treat It Like Public Health (Your "Financial Cocaine" frame)

7) Advertising and influencer bans

Ban:
- celebrity endorsements,
- influencer promotion,
- "guaranteed returns,"
- romance-scam adjacent solicitation,
- affiliate commissions for referrals.

Require warning labels on any allowed exposure products:

"Irreversible transfers. High fraud environment. No deposit insurance. Total loss possible."

8) Mandatory "cooling-off" and suitability rules (if not a total ban)

If policymakers won't fully ban immediately:

- 30-day cooling period for first purchase,
- hard caps for retail deposits,
- suitability tests (like options trading),
- prohibition for seniors over a certain age unless advised by a fiduciary (controversial but effective).

D. Enforcement: make it real

9) Create a dedicated Crypto Harm Task Force

Cross-agency:

- consumer protection,
- financial regulators,
- DOJ,
- Treasury/FinCEN,
- cybercrime units.

Measure success using:

- quarterly scam losses,
- elder victim losses,
- recovery rate,
- ransomware payment incidence.

10) Criminalize "facilitation infrastructure"

Target enablers:

- mixer operators that launder retail scam proceeds,
- fake exchange operators,
- "pig-butchering" networks and call centers,
- mule networks cashing out victims' funds.

E. International coordination (or the ban leaks)

11) Treaty-style cooperation

Push allies to align on:

- platform blacklists,
- rapid freeze requests,
- standardized evidence sharing,

- cross-border seizure frameworks.

A retail ban is far stronger when neighbors enforce similar standards.

F. Replace the "need" so people don't feel trapped

12) Offer safe alternatives

To prevent backlash and underground demand, expand:

- instant low-fee bank transfers,
- regulated mobile payments,
- cheap remittances through licensed rails,
- clear guidance that digital payment $\neq$ crypto.

- "This is consumer protection and elder protection."
- "This is anti-scam and anti-ransomware."
- "We are banning a high-harm product—not banning technology."
- "Money must be recoverable. Fraud must be stoppable."

timeline :

Phase 1 (0–90 days): advertising + influencer ban; licensing freeze; block bank rails to unlicensed platforms.

Phase 2 (3–9 months): retail trading ban + custody ban; liability regime; reversibility requirement.

Phase 3 (9–18 months): enforcement scale-up; international alignment; alternative payment upgrades.

www.ingramcontent.com/pod-product-compliance
Lightning Source LLC
Chambersburg PA
CBHW071737200326
41519CB00021BC/6763